Southwestern PENNSYLVANIA

LAND OF OPPORTUNITY

Written by **Vince Gagetta**
Corporate profiles by **Peter Longini & Kathleen Ganster**
Featuring the photography of **Kevin R. Cooke, Graule Studios**

Southwestern PENNSYLVANIA
LAND OF OPPORTUNITY

By Vince Gagetta
Corporate Profiles by Peter R. Longini and Kathleen Ganster
Featuring the Photography of Kevin R. Cooke of Graule Studios

Staff for *Southwestern Pennsylvania: Land of Opportunity*

Sales Associates:	**Sheli L. Ferrand, Richard M. Hadley, Lynn Ambrosiani**
Executive Editor:	**James E. Turner**
Managing Editor:	**Wendi L. Lewis**
Design Director:	**Scott Phillips**
Designers:	**Scott Phillips and Eddie Lavoie**
Production Artist:	**Kimberly A. Smith**
Photo Editors:	**Eddie Lavoie and Wendi Lewis**
Production Managers:	**Cindy Lovett and Jarrod Stiff**
Editorial Assistant:	**Katrina Williams**
Sales Assistant:	**Annette Lozier**
Proofreader:	**Angela K. Mann**
Accounting Services:	**Sara Ann Turner**
Printing Production:	**Frank Rosenburg/T.V. Allen**

CCI

Community Communications, Inc.
Montgomery, Alabama

James E. Turner, *Chairman of the Board*
Ronald P. Beers, *President*
Daniel S. Chambliss, *Vice President*

Preface

I never used to think about Southwestern Pennsylvania being a Land of Opportunity. To me, that was how places with spectacular economies and robust job markets (and, often, climates to die for) were described, which certainly did not fit my wildest notion of the Pittsburgh Region. But Land of Opportunity is what Lawrence Maloney, managing director of the Association of Iron and Steel Engineers, called the region during one of my early interviews for this book. The reference was so casual, so off-the-cuff, that I could tell he really meant it. This was not self-serving puffery; this was a straightforward, honest observation. And it floored me.

I have to say that my reaction to the Land of Opportunity description would have been almost universally shared by my fellow Pittsburghers (and everyone in the ten-county area is a Pittsburgher, whether living in the central city or in the region's farthest corners). We are, most of us, unreconstructed realists, never mind that our love of and loyalty to the area and our resistance to leaving it, even when other places beckon with better jobs and, yes, more pleasant climates, are as unrealistic as they are legendary.

I was so taken aback hearing the place where I was born, raised, educated, and have witnessed slip from its glory years as an industrial and economic behemoth described in such an unfamiliarly positive way that I decided that I had to seriously re-examine my preconceived notions of the region's weaknesses and strengths and to reconsider my foregone conclusion (shared by many of my neighbors) that the former far outnumbered the latter. I am thankful that I got that wake-up call, because my subsequent research and interviews convinced me that Southwestern Pennsylvania has a lot more going for it than I and many Pittsburghers imagined. Of course, we all knew that the area consistently scores high in livability and life-quality rankings, that both housing prices and crime rates are low, and that Pittsburgh is one of the cleanest and friendliest cities in the country.

We long have been proud of the region's abundant recreational and cultural opportunities: state, county, and local parks are ubiquitous and well patronized; there are more private pleasure boats licensed on the region's rivers than anywhere in the U.S. except Dade County, Florida; there are more than fifty museums in the region, including the largest in the world devoted to a single artist, native son Andy Warhol; and Allegheny County's public library system is one of largest in world. And I knew there have been a lot of movies made in the area recently. But I didn't realize that movie making pumps about $183 million a year into the region's economy and the area has become one of the country's top-ten documentary film centers.

I also didn't know how much progress has been made in the past few years in stabilizing the economy, attracting new companies, and creating more jobs. So it took me a while to realize that there are, indeed, opportunities enough here to allow the region to describe itself as a land full of them.

What kind of opportunities? Well, jobs for one, particularly in high-tech industries. I learned, for example, that thirty thousand new jobs have been created in the region in the last three years, that high-tech companies now employ one of every ten workers in region, and that the region's fastest growing public companies are all computer related. I discovered that there now are 450 software firms in the region, which makes it the sixth largest software employment center in the U.S.; that the ten counties are home to 850 firms that manufacture products or develop processes for cleaning up air and water pollution and 700 companies in the biomedical, biotechnology, and life science fields; and that some 170 research facilities are located in the region. So it is hardly surprising that the region is ranked fifth in the country for research and development, ninth for small business development, and twelfth for high-tech job growth.

The presence here of two of the country's highly rated research universities, Carnegie-Mellon and the University of Pittsburgh, has contributed mightily to the region's success in developing a high-tech economy, as have the twenty-seven other colleges and universities in Southwestern Pennsylvania that enroll almost one hundred thousand students and the 100-or-so vocational-technical training schools enrolling almost thirty thousand.

High tech gets most of the job-creation headlines but I learned that the industries that long were the region's economic foundation are again making their presence felt: manufacturing is making a real comeback in parts of the region, steel making has returned (even if only on a relatively modest scale), and coal mining continues play a prominent role (the world's most productive underground mine is located in Greene County).

I was pleased to learn that the state, after several years of what seemed to most Pittsburghers to be benign neglect, has dramatically increased funding for projects in the region, most notably the commitment of $338 million to the Mon-Fayette Expressway, which will run from West Virginia to Pittsburgh and is the most expensive highway construction project in Pennsylvania history; $150 million to expand the Lawrence Convention Center in Pittsburgh; and $38 million to help the University of Pittsburgh build a convocation center.

And Governor Tom Ridge added icing to the state funding cake in July 1998 when he announced a program to distribute $40 million throughout the ten-county region for sixteen mostly industrial development projects. Those projects are expected to help create twenty-one thousand new jobs over the next ten years and attract more than $500 million in private investment.

All of the foregoing should be enough to convince the most hidebound skeptic that the Pittsburgh region need not be shy about proclaiming itself a Land of Opportunity. It convinced me, and I am not one easily convinced.

-Vince Gagetta

Table of Contents

Chapter

1

Allegheny County

istory is being made in Allegheny County. The system that has governed the county since before the U.S. Constitution was ratified is being replaced. Beginning in the year 2000, the county will be governed by an elected county executive and a fifteen-member elected county council, with an appointed county manager in charge of day-to-day operations, and not by a board of three elected commissioners.

The change is more significant than it may initially appear and could prove to be staggering in importance. Not only is a system more than two centuries old (it went into effect when the county was created on September 24, 1788) being replaced, but more importantly the new system gives residents privileges they never had before—like proposing and voting on referendums and petitioning the government to consider specific laws. That will put a whole new spin on how matters related to spending, taxation, and representation are handled in the county.

Such populist input likely will have an enormous impact on economic development decisions in Allegheny County as well. Had the new system already been in place, for example, it is unlikely that two new professional sports stadiums would be being built in Pittsburgh—at least not with the help of county tax money. In May 1998, voters in Allegheny and the region's nine other counties rejected a sales-tax increase to fund stadium construction and other projects. But the majority Allegheny County commissioners and the mayor of Pittsburgh rescued the stadium projects by devising "Plan B," an alternate approach that uses existing county tax revenues, not new taxes, to help pay the bill. Under Plan B, $13.4 million in county tax revenues are allocated annually to pay off a $330 million bond issue that provides a major chunk of the projects' financing. (The remaining $470 million of the projects' estimated $800 million cost will come from the state, the football and baseball teams, private investors, and the federal government.)

Allegheny County is making history with a new form of government, reflecting the forward-thinking intentions of her people. Photo by Kevin Cooke/Graule Studios

If they had had the referendum and petitioning privileges granted under the new government system, Allegheny County residents (if the letters-to-the-editor columns of the local newspapers are any indication) likely would have blocked the use of any county tax funds, new or otherwise, for the stadium projects.

Pittsburgh International Airport, sixteen miles from downtown Pittsburgh in Findlay Township, is considered one of the world's most modern terminal complexes. Photo by Kevin Cooke/Graule Studios

But residents probably would have approved another component of Plan B: the $267 million expansion of the David L. Lawrence Convention Center in Pittsburgh's downtown. Few disagree that the center's expansion and modernization are critical to attracting larger conventions and larger groups of conventioneers to the city and county, spur a needed increase in the number of hotel and motel rooms throughout the county, and boost economic development efforts.

The Plan B projects are included on a list of thirty-five publicly and privately financed projects currently at various stages of development in the county. According to the Allegheny County Department of Economic Development, those projects, estimated to cost about $3 billion, could create more than thirty thousand new jobs. That certainly would brighten the economic outlook for Allegheny County, which, along with the rest of Southwestern Pennsylvania, has yet to fully recover from the virtual demise in the 1980s of the heavy industries that had been the region's economic life blood for generations.

The shutting down of so many manufacturing plants and the loss of so many jobs would be a severe blow to any area's economy. It was particularly so in Allegheny County, whose industrial heritage can be traced to colonial days.

The area first became a manufacturing center because it had an abundance of natural resources and was strategically located just west of the Allegheny Mountains, which then were an awesome barrier separating the more developed east from the frontier. Manufacturing flourished in what are now Pittsburgh and Allegheny County because it was difficult and costly to import goods from the east over primitive mountain roads. So things needed by local settlers and those passing through (after the Revolutionary War, Pittsburgh became the key outfitting post for settlers heading west, thus its claim of being Gateway to the West) were made locally: initially glass, furniture, and iron tools, and also the boats that were needed to transport goods. And all the county's manufacturing facilities were fueled by locally mined coal—indeed, coal mining was an important source of jobs in Allegheny County for many years.

Allegheny County has an abundance of natural resources, and a stunning view of the Allegheny Mountains. Photo by Kevin Cooke/Graule Studios

Boat building was Allegheny County's first industry. It was not long after the area was settled that the building of barges, keelboats, and even ocean-going ships began along the Allegheny, Monongahela, and Ohio rivers.

The first glass was made in the area in 1795 and the first large-scale production of plate glass in the nation began in Creighton in 1883. Glassworks flourished, and Allegheny County once produced more than a quarter of all the glass made in the country.

Iron making became the county's (and the region's) principal industry more than 185 years ago during the War of 1812. During the Civil War, the area earned the title Arsenal of the Union for producing the cannons, iron-clad ships, and rail cars that figured prominently in the Union's victory.

It took a couple of decades and the genius of one man, Andrew Carnegie, to transform the Arsenal of the Union into the Steel Capital of the World. Carnegie, the son of Scottish immigrants who grew up poor in what now is Pittsburgh's North Side, helped the cause by, among other things, adopting cost-saving technologies like the Bessemer Process. And he teamed with Henry Clay Frick, who owned the coke works in Westmoreland County that fueled Carnegie's mills, to build an industrial empire with Pittsburgh and Allegheny County as its center. (In 1901 Carnegie and Frick

formed the world's first billion-dollar corporation, United States Steel.)

That industrial empire supported Allegheny County's economy well into the 1980s, until steel's decline. Manufacturing, once the county's preeminent employment category, now accounts for slightly more than 10 percent of the jobs in the county. Still, 10 percent is a great improvement over the figures from a few years ago. Also heartening: almost 20 percent of the county's manufacturing jobs are in primary metals, the industry that made the area an industrial powerhouse.

Manufacturing ranks behind service, which accounts for almost 38 percent of all county jobs (with fully a third of them in health care), and retailing, which stands at almost 19 percent. Finance and insurance, transportation and public utilities, wholesaling, and construction also are important job generators.

Advanced technology businesses finally are making their presence more strongly felt in the county. The county's high-tech successes are attributable in large measure to small firms related, however remotely in some cases, to Pittsburgh's research universities or to the schools' technological initiatives (as is covered in some detail in the chapter on Pittsburgh). But success in profitable

technological areas is not confined to start-ups and academically related ventures. Many of the county's larger and long established companies also are making important contributions by developing products and processes in the fields of environmental protection, advanced materials, chemicals, factory automation, computers, and biotechnology.

In its glory years, Pittsburgh was America's third largest corporate headquarters city. Moves and mergers have changed that but still today eight Fortune 500 companies call Pittsburgh and Allegheny County home: USX Corporation, Alcoa, H.J. Heinz, PPG Industries, PNC Bank, Mellon Bank Corporation, Allegheny Teledyne, and CNG. And a number of European, Asian, and Canadian companies have established their United States headquarters in Allegheny County.

Many companies, large and small, long-established and start-ups alike, remain in the county or are attracted to the county for the same reasons people are: quality of life concerns. Housing is

It was not long after the area was settled that the building of barges, keelboats, and even ocean-going ships began along the Allegheny, Monongahela, and Ohio Rivers. Photo by Kevin Cooke/Graule Studios

affordable, the crime rate is low, and the quality of health care is exceptional. Educational opportunities are both plentiful and outstanding: eight colleges and universities are located in the county as are several satellite campus of out-of-town schools. And the Community College of Allegheny County, the largest community college in Pennsylvania, operates four campuses and also holds classes in eight off-camps centers and four hundred sites throughout the county.

There are numerous cultural, artistic, and recreational opportunities for residents and visitors. There are fourteen public parks in the county. Nine of them are county owned and operated, the other five are Pittsburgh city parks.

Construction is a sure sign of growth, and an indicator of the county's role as a leading choice for the relocation of both businesses and families. Photo by Kevin Cooke/Graule Studios

The Port Authority of Allegheny County operates more than seven hundred buses daily, a 22.5-mile light rail system that features a downtown Pittsburgh subway, and the oldest and steepest incline in the United States. (The Port Authority leases a second incline to a private non-profit group which maintains a daily schedule.)

Pittsburgh International Airport, sixteen miles from downtown Pittsburgh in Findlay Township, opened in 1992 and is considered to be one of the world's most modern terminal complexes. It served more than 21 million passengers in 1997. Because it makes such a favorable impression on air travelers to the area, the airport is one of Allegheny County's most valuable and most valued assets. It will play a more prominent role in the county's economic revitalization efforts soon, as the old airport's terminal, not far from the new airport, is demolished and a business park, air cargo facility, aviation

center, hotel, and related facilities are built on the site. Estimated cost of the project: almost \$369 million.

These airport improvements are typical of the grand-scale projects Allegheny County is pursuing in its effort to invigorate its economy, attract new companies and new jobs, and help its established companies grow and become more profitable. Recently, the county's and the city of Pittsburgh's economic development departments were merged and now what for many years were competing departments with competing agendas are a single entity with a single focus. Most local observers see the merger as a first, very positive step forward and are confident that it will result in the kinds of creative, far-reaching, and realistic economic development strategies and initiatives that the county and the city both must have to compete more vigorously in an increasingly competitive economic marketplace. ₧

Indiana University of Pennsylvania
in Pittsburgh and Allegheny County

Indiana University of Pennsylvania, whose campus in Indiana County serves more than thirteen thousand students, is among the state's largest institutions of higher education. But its academic reach extends far beyond its main campus. Just since 1994, IUP has entered into exchange agreements with universities in Costa Rica, Jordan, Bratislava, Colombia, Mexico, Turkey, Spain, Germany, and the United Kingdom.

Closer to home, the University has also conducted an aggressive outreach program. In addition to its main campus in Indiana, IUP now operates satellite branches in Kittanning and Punxsutawney. More recently, the University has taken a closer look at addressing Pittsburgh's unmet educational needs. There, it has found a variety of opportunities to build a presence and enrich its offerings.

Just outside Pittsburgh, in the suburb of Monroeville, an IUP Graduate and Professional Center now offers these two-year Master's Degree programs, with evening and weekend classes designed for the working professional:
- Executive M.B.A.
- M.A. in Adult and Community Education
- M.A. in Criminology
- M.A. in Industrial and Labor Relations
- M.A. in Education

Leveraging its traditional strength in teacher education and training, IUP's College of Education has formed a student teaching partnership with Pittsburgh's public schools. An Urban Student Teaching Center at one Pittsburgh high school, and a faculty assessment program at another, are also elements of their partnership.

At the same time, IUP was awarded a grant to finance an innovative program to recruit and retain minority teachers for Pittsburgh's city schools. Under a separate arrangement, IUP and the Community College of Allegheny County

formed a partnership that enables students seeking four-year degrees in elementary education to complete their course requirements without traveling to IUP's main campus for classes.

Other Pittsburgh-related initiatives by IUP involve different University specialties. For example, in collaboration with Pittsburgh's Bureau of Police Training, IUP is offering a variety of classes in Criminal Justice. A Pittsburgh training center, designed to reduce health risks for workers employed in industries handling hazardous wastes, was formed through a partnership of IUP with management and labor organizations in the affected industries.

Through a pilot project with Pittsburgh's National City Bank, IUP became the test site for a high-technology identification card which simultaneously provides key access to dormitories, long-distance telephone service, vending machine purchases, library book circulation, and admission to restricted events as well as standard credit and debit services. And an IUP safety consultation service, in cooperation with state and federal safety agencies, is helping small business throughout the Pittsburgh area to address potential hazards and avoid

IUP operates satellite campuses in Kittanning, Punxsutawney and the city of Pittsburgh.

costly OSHA citations.

IUP has also formed a number of health-related partnerships in the Pittsburgh area. They include an arrangement with Western Pennsylvania Hospital in respiratory care training; with Allegheny General Hospital in attracting prospective physicians to family practice; and with Gateway Rehabilitation Center in developing training focused on chemical dependency programs.

To cement its ties to the region's largest city, IUP has opened an office in the heart of Pittsburgh's central business district. The new space, located in the ALCOA Building, houses an evolving combination of functions and helps to confirm IUP's emerging role as one of Pittsburgh's leading academic institutions. **Pa**

| Photo by Kevin Cooke/Graule   Studios

Chapter

2

Armstrong County

A road and a river are helping Armstrong County live up to its recently coined claim of being "The Best Thing Next To Pittsburgh."

The road is the Allegheny Valley Expressway, Pennsylvania Route 28, a four-lane, limited-access highway directly linking Armstrong County and the county seat, Kittanning, with downtown Pittsburgh. The expressway and the access it provides have helped the county achieve a modest population increase in recent years.

The river is the Allegheny, navigable for all of the fifty-one miles that it travels through the county on its way to downtown Pittsburgh, where it joins with the Monongahela to create the Ohio River.

The road and the river link Armstrong County and the region's commercial, economic, and cultural hub in Pittsburgh. And county officials are positioning the road and the river along with continuing development of the county-owned and operated industrial park system as the key elements of an aggressive campaign to lure new people, new business, and new jobs to the county.

There is room for all three. Armstrong is a largely undeveloped, relatively unspoiled county where fully 85 percent of its 73,872 residents live in what are categorized as rural areas and where the county's Visitors Guide proudly and justifiably proclaims that its "most popular attraction is its scenery."

The Allegheny Valley Expressway plays a most important role in the economic development campaign. To lend credence to their "next best thing" slogan, county officials point out that during off-peak hours, it takes only about fifty minutes to drive the forty-two mostly traffic-signal-free miles southwest from Kittanning, which is virtually at the geographic center of the county, to the heart of downtown Pittsburgh's Golden Triangle. They also have targeted an area

Armstrong County's Visitors Guide proudly and justifiably proclaims that this county's "most popular attraction is its scenery." Photo by Kevin Cooke/Graule Studios

just off the expressway and just north of Armstrong's border with Allegheny County, the county that includes the city of Pittsburgh, as the site of its newest and largest county-owned industrial park.

The completion of the expressway (a several-mile-long link about halfway between Pittsburgh and Kittanning sat unfinished for several years) has allowed Armstrong officials to, in their words, "get serious about economic development and begin to market the county more aggressively."

The economic development campaign, begun in earnest in 1991, has borne fruit. In the past half-dozen years, about forty companies and more than thirteen hundred new, mostly service-sector jobs have found their way into the county.

More of both are on the way, county officials are convinced—lured by a very attractive tax structure, what are reported to be the lowest utility rates in Pennsylvania, land costs that are significantly lower than many other areas in the region, and a stable, skilled, and eager labor pool. The labor pool's stability and not a little of its eagerness are products, most observers believe, of the county's rural environment with its laid back and relaxed lifestyle, low crime rate, affordable housing, sound education system (The Pennsylvania State University, Indiana University of Pennsylvania, and Butler County Community College each offer college-level instruction in the county), and abundant recreational opportunities.

Recreational opportunities are what attract many visitors to the county, particularly from Pittsburgh and the region's other more populated areas but also from throughout western Pennsylvania. The Allegheny River long has been the county's premier recreational attraction, especially for boaters and fishing enthusiasts.

The Allegheny River is the county's premier recreational attraction, drawing boating and fishing enthusiasts from throughout the area. Photo courtesy Armstrong County Planning & Development

The Allegheny has every species of fish found in Pennsylvania and is considered to be probably the best river in the eastern United States for catching walleyed pike.

In Kittanning, the Allegheny serves as the backdrop of the town's Riverfront Park. Considered by many to be one of the most beautiful waterfronts in western Pennsylvania, the park occupies more than four thousand feet of continuous riverfront. A riverfront strip that large that does not contain railroad tracks or water-dependent industrial plants is a rarity in this part of Pennsylvania.

Armstrong County offers peaceful, cost-efficient rural living within an easy commuting distance of the big city of Pittsburgh, giving residents the best of both worlds. Photo by Kevin Cooke/Graule Studios

The Allegheny River is the key element in Armstrong County's tourism promotion program but it certainly is not the only element. The county also boasts three large lakes covering more than 1,600 total acres: Crooked Creek, Keystone, and Mahoning Creek; numerous warm- and cold-water fishing creeks and streams; five state game lands with more than 5,300 acres open to public hunting; more than 100,000 acres of private land open to hunting under the county's Farm/Game Program; 113 public and private parks; 200 miles of trails

for hiking and bicycling; six golf courses; several well-maintained campgrounds; and three YMCAs. The Belmont Complex in West Kittanning, one of the county's largest recreational facilities, offers ice skating, hockey, and skating lessons, and has the county's largest outdoor swimming pool.

A sizable number of those who initially come to Armstrong from more crowded areas of the region for the boating, fishing, hunting, hiking, and other leisure-time pursuits have been known to succumb to the lure of easier country living and have decided to make the county their permanent, year-round home. And now that the Allegheny Valley Expressway has trimmed commuting time to Pittsburgh to a tolerable amount, their number may well increase, as more

of those outdoor-sports enthusiasts come to realize that they can enjoy less stressful, less costly rural living without putting themselves out of reach of the career, professional, and cultural opportunities the city provides.

The decrease in commuting time to Pittsburgh and Allegheny County also opens up new job and career opportunities for Armstrong residents who, traditionally, have been content to work near to where they live. Currently, more than 60 percent of employed Armstrong residents work in the county. That number could well decrease over time as residents realize that other work opportunities may exist about an hour or less from home.

That is an option that has to be attractive to a large number of Armstrong residents, especially those in the prime earning and career-building years. The county has them in considerable numbers. Almost 30 percent of the residents are between the ages of 25 and 44, and another 13 percent or so are in the 15-to-24 age bracket. They are the county's future, a future that depends on their being able to take advantage of meaningful job and career opportunities within Armstrong's borders and in readily accessible areas outside the county.

Providing such opportunities is a serious challenge in a county—and a region—that have yet to recover fully from the catastrophic economic downturn of the 1980s, when most of the mills, factories, and mines that were the backbone of the area's economy either shut their doors or seriously cut back on employment.

Back then, mining and manufacturing were the county's preeminent sources of employment and provided good, steady, well-paying—if often very dangerous—job opportunities. Today, manufacturing accounts for less than 18 percent of Armstrong County's nonagricultural jobs and mining only about 5 percent, according to Pennsylvania Department of Labor and Industry records. Only one manufacturing company and one coal mining company are listed among the county's ten biggest employers. More county residents are engaged in the wholesale and retail trades (24 percent) and service-related employment (22 percent) than in manufacturing. And there are as many residents working for

Mahoning Dam helps the county generate power as well as moderating water levels. Photo courtesy Armstrong County Planning and Development Office

local, state, and federal government bodies as there are in manufacturing.

Those are somber comparisons to make when describing a place with such a rich and strong industrial tradition, a place where many of the region's and the nation's most vitally important and dominant industries were spawned or nurtured: mining, iron and steel production, brick making, lumbering, and glass making.

Iron was made in the county at Bradys Bend twenty years before there was a single blast furnace in Pittsburgh. The first iron rails made west of the Allegheny Mountains were produced at Bradys Bend. There were fifteen blast furnaces in operation in Armstrong County by 1881.

In 1873, the Rogers and Burchfield Mill in Leechburg was the first in the world to use natural gas to fuel an ironmaking operation. A year later, the plant became the first in the world to make black plate, tin, and ternplate.

Ford City is considered to be the home of the United States' plate glass industry. The Ford City Glass Factory, founded by Captain John B. Ford, was in its day the largest plant of its kind in the world.

The Daugherty Visible Typewriter, the first-ever visible typewriter, was invented by J.D. Daugherty of Kittanning and was manufactured there for many years.

Those were the types of enterprises that were the foundation upon which Armstrong County built a strong and vibrant industrial economy, a foundation that helped make the county and the entire Greater Pittsburgh region an industrial and economic powerhouse. Neither the county nor the region likely will regain the positions of industrial dominance they once commanded, but they have not abandoned their hopes and plans for a brighter, more stable economic future.

Armstrong officials are counting on continuing development of the county's industrial/business park system and further development of the Allegheny Valley Expressway to lure more companies and more jobs, particularly in manufacturing, to the area. The county owns and operates three industrial/business parks and a small-business incubator, has a fourth park under construction, and currently plans to develop two more. There also are two privately owned industrial parks in the county.

The newest county-owned park is planned for Slate Lick, just a few miles north of

Armstrong is a largely undeveloped, relatively unspoiled county that is a paradise for outdoor and wildlife enthusiasts. Photo courtesy Armstrong County Planning and Development Office

Armstrong's border with Allegheny County—and right alongside the Allegheny Valley Expressway. Slate Lick will not be a traditional industrial/business park; more than half of its 850 acres will be occupied by housing, retail outlets, and recreational facilities. County officials think this so-called "live, work, and play" concept, which already has been successfully implemented in other areas, neatly fits the character of the county. It is a development approach, they feel, that likely will appeal to and attract the types of companies and the type of people who are comfortable in a place like Armstrong County. ▪

Armstrong County Chamber of Commerce

With more than 650 square miles of woods, fields and rivers, Armstrong County is both serene and picturesque. More than 113 public and private recreational sites of every type allow residents and visitors alike to take advantage of those scenic resources. But Armstrong County is also the site of an energetic and growing businesses community. Serving these businesses for more than 75 years has been the Armstrong County Chamber of Commerce.

Chartered in 1922 as the Kittanning Chamber of Commerce, the organization's original mission was described as "marketing, fostering, and developing the commercial, manufacturing, financial, and general interests of the community." Through the years, the organization expanded to become the Armstrong County Chamber of Commerce. Today, more than 200 members from the county's business, manufacturing, agricultural, retail, educational, and service industries support the Chamber's revised and updated mission: "to support and strengthen the business, professional, and industrial communities; to encourage the development of new enterprises; and to advocate for our membership."

According to Patricia Kirkpatrick, Executive Director of the Chamber, "We are here to serve our members. The Board is committed to providing the services our members need and to having an open dialogue so we understand exactly what it is they want." Whatever assistance a member business requires, the Chamber attempts to provide it. As a result, the Chamber offers a wealth of services and information, ranging from legislative forums and regulatory information, to marketing sources and new business opportunities.

Securing discounted services, identifying educational resources, and providing networking opportunities are also basic

to the Chamber's service mix. For businesses, as well as for individuals considering relocation to Armstrong County, the Chamber provides relocation packages, demographic packages, and maps.

"The Chamber provides a wide range of opportunities for networking that are important to businesses. They also provide certain services available only to members, and discounts on other services," observes Liz White, a past President of the Chamber and currently a member of its Board of Directors. White is also Secretary/Treasurer of White Enterprises, located in Kittanning. "I have personally found the Chamber's services to be of great value," she said.

The Chamber supports a variety of community activities and events such as art exhibits, festivals, fairs, and races. It also hosts special events including "Business After Hours" receptions, a Victorian Christmas Dinner, informational events, and charitable fund-raisers. A Chamber-produced cable television show

The Armstrong County Chamber of Commerce is active in promoting the area as a great place to live, work, and raise a family.

is carried in the Kittanning/Ford City area on the second Tuesday of each month. In addition, the Armstrong Chamber co-hosts events with its counterparts throughout the region.

"We work with neighboring chambers so that we function as a cooperative unit instead of as competing organizations. We work together to strengthen the economic development of our area," said White.

The Armstrong County Chamber of Commerce constantly seeks new opportunities to serve its members. "Our new logo is two hands shaking in partnership. That is what we are for our members: their business partner. We are always looking for new ways to support and strengthen the businesses of Armstrong County," said Kirkpatrick.

Armstrong County Memorial Hospital

"A Century of Caring" which Armstrong County Memorial Hospital marked on October 5, 1998 embraced an era of change so far-reaching that not even the most visionary dreamers of the 19th century could have imagined them. No aspect of society, technology or medical practice was left untouched. Yet despite repeated changes in name, location and governance, this hospital's dedication to serving its rural home community never wavered.

When it was chartered in 1898, the hospital—then known as the Kittanning Hospital—was just a hastily-equipped infirmary in a downtown store room. There, itinerant railroad workers stricken with typhoid fever or injured in construction accidents received compassion and treatment.

It was a time in which many households still relied on superstition and bogus elixers to cure whatever ailed them. Physicians of the day were generalists, typically performing surgery as well as dispensing advise and medicine to patients of all ages and conditions. When a family needed a doctor, the doctor came to the home. Hospitals were where their patients went when hope was gone.

But the founders of Kittanning Hospital knew better. In 1899, they purchased and modified a large house, which became a 35-bed hospital served by a six-person staff. In 1901, most patients paid $7.50 a week and stayed an average of 30 days. As demand grew—900 patients were admitted in 1921—so did the need for a new facility. However, it wasn't until 1936 that a new 60-bed facility, now re-named Armstrong County Hospital, finally opened to patients.

A series of expansions and modernizations followed throughout the years. But by 1969, when the hospital admitted more than 8,000 patients, it became clear keeping pace with demand for services and advances in health care required an

entirely new facility. "We had no board specialties before that time, and if you looked at the future of medicine, that was really the only way to go," former hospital board president Dick Laube observed. "If we didn't have a modern facility, we couldn't attract board-certified physicians."

The new facility—now known as Armstrong County Memorial Hospital to honor the community's war dead—opened on a 175-acre hilltop site in May of 1973. With 217 patient rooms and ample support facilities, the new facility boasted four fully-outfitted operating rooms, a post-operative recovery room, and an ICU, as well as specialized procedure areas for nuclear medicine, radiation therapy, mammography, orthopedics, and more.

Its medical personnel grew to include more than 120 physicians representing a wide range of specialties. The nursing staff of 275 includes 130 registered nurses. And its medical professionals are supported by another 200 ancillary personnel.

Today, the hospital's mission remains sharply focused on cancer care, psychiatric counseling, physical therapy, and

TOP: In 1998, Armstrong County Hospital celebrated "a Century of Caring."

BOTTOM: Chartered in 1898 as the Kittanning Hospital, early services included compassionate treatment of the ailments and injuries suffered by itinerant railroad workers.

cardiac treatment. Three satellite clinics run by the hospital now serve the county's outlying areas. Additionally, a wide range of education, training, and home-based outpatient services—echoing the hospital's earliest days—now complement its extensive inpatient programs. **Pa**

ALLTEL

Who is wiring Southwestern Pennsylvania's scenic rural communities into the 21st century? In Kittanning, Meadville, Murrysville, and Ridgeway, as well as dozens of other small towns and boroughs throughout the area, the answer is ALLTEL—an $8.6 billion communications company with more than 5.6 million customers and operations in 22 states.

While local telephone service to more than 200,000 homes and businesses in Pennsylvania forms the foundation of ALLTEL's growing presence in the region, it represents only the most visible element of a much larger array of sophisticated telecommunication services that the company provides.

In rural Greene County, for example, students from five school districts and one vocational school are taking classes from Waynesburg College. But they are doing so without ever leaving their own school classrooms. How? ALLTEL is pro-

ALLTEL combines the capabilities of cellular, paging, and advanced data messaging services that, together, form the sort of powerful package that has become critical to serving rural customers.

viding fully interactive video conferencing to all of the affected locations. Their success in distance learning has prompted school superintendents throughout the county to look into ways of expanding the system even further.

In Meadville, Allegheny College has designated ALLTEL as its sole source for local, long-distance and Internet access through the year 2008. In addition to wiring the college's dormitory rooms into a local area network offering a comprehensive assortment of high-speed services, the agreement also provides the college's faculty and off-campus students with a leading-edge electronic service package.

In Erie, ALLTEL's telephone directory publishing unit puts out 340 different phone books every year to serve the company's customers in various operating areas. Altogether, these books represent approximately a million separate listings.

Outside of Pennsylvania, ALLTEL has emerged as one of the nation's leading providers of wireless phone service, with some of their areas using the all-digital PCS high-frequency bands. That technology combines the capabilities of cellular, paging, and advanced data messaging services. Together, they form the sort of powerful package that has become critical to serving ALLTEL's predominantly rural customers.

Although ALLTEL's telephone services, which include the full array of local and long-distance transmission technologies, are the most widely recognized aspects of its business, they are not the only ones. Technical solutions crafted by ALLTEL engineers are enabling doctors in widely separate locations to confer in real time by

Local telephone service to more than 200,000 homes and businesses in Pennsylvania forms the foundation of ALLTEL's growing presence in the region.

sharing patient files and X-rays over the Internet. A leading forest products company maintains contact with its workforce scattered across more than a million acres of wilderness. And a county jail in Florida is now able to arraign prisoners remotely by video—no matter where they may have been hiding.

The company also operates an information services division whose custom software products cater to customers in the finance and telecommunications industries. Project management, customer service call center operation, mortgage loan processing, electronic commerce, and customer billing are among the rapidly growing family of sophisticated business solutions offered by ALLTEL.

Regardless of whether the customer is a bank in Australia, a phone company in Manila, or a farm in Armstrong County, ALLTEL is committed to combining the greatest value, the latest technology, and the fullest integration of communication services available anywhere. **Pa**

Snyder Associated Companies, Inc.

In June of 1941, as the clouds of war began to gather, two brothers—Elmer A. and Charles H. Snyder, Sr. of Kittanning— joined forces to form a small construction company. Little did they suspect that during the next five decades, their business would expand to include mining, natural gas and oil, manufacturing, agriculture, banking, and wholesale distribution. But today, three generations of the Snyder family as well as hundreds of others, work in the collection of ventures now known as Snyder Associated Companies, Inc.

It happened in stages. Southwestern Pennsylvania is coal country. So in 1945, the Snyders expanded their activities into coal mining. Three years later, they purchased Glacial Sand & Gravel Company. That same year, Chuck Snyder, Jr., a second-generation family member, joined the family business.

Nineteen fifty-one marked a year of growth for the brothers. They opened the Quality Inn Royle Motel located on Route 422 near Kittanning. At the same time, they also expanded outside of Pennsylvania by purchasing the Highway Equipment & Supply in Orlando, Florida. Allegheny Mineral Corporation was created in 1953 to quarry limestone. The Bauer Block Company, which manufactures concrete blocks, septic tanks, and other cement products, was purchased in 1974.

Snyder Associated Companies, Inc., headquartered in Kittanning, was formed in 1976 to manage the firm's growing family of subsidiaries. Diversification has been key to its success. That diversity continues. Logan Candy Company, Inc.—a Butler County wholesale and retail of distributor of candy, tobacco, and grocery products— was added in 1984. In 1988, Armstrong Cement & Supply

Corporation of Cabot, Pennsylvania, joined the businesses.

Using the proceeds of their diverse companies, the family created the Snyder Charitable Foundation in June of 1987 to finance various philanthropic projects and assist non-profit agencies. Mark Snyder, Elmer's son and current Corporate Secretary, put it this way: "I grew up in the Boy Scouts. One of the components in scouting is community service. Plus, my family has always believed in giving back to the community whether it be through donations to various projects or creating new business to

Founders from left: Chuck and Elmer Snyder

provide employment and strengthen the economy."

Throughout the years, other family members also joined the corporation. Today, a host of Snyder family members work in its various companies. "We have a very good relationship. Each of us is focused on running successful businesses. We make our own decisions, our own mistakes, and can achieve our own successes," explained Mark Snyder. "But we can also draw on the expertise and strengths of our family members."

Today, Snyder Associated Companies, Inc. employs 350-400 people in Butler, Indiana, and Armstrong counties. Lifelong residents of Pennsylvania, both of the company's founders remain active in the business. Charles Sr., now 90, works part-time during the summer months, and Elmer, 82, works every day except when wintering in Florida. Theirs is a company built on a solid foundation of commitment to family and community. 𝐏𝐚

25 cubic yard walking dragline

Armstrong County Industrial Development Authority

Businesses hoping to build, relocate, or expand in Armstrong County have a powerful ally—the Armstrong County Industrial Development Authority (ACIDA). ACIDA assists businesses from their initial planning stages through to full commercial operation.

"We work as a clearinghouse to provide information and assistance to businesses. We like to refer to ourselves as a 'one stop shop' for them," said Rich Palilla, Executive Director of ACIDA.

According to Palilla, companies are looking for an agency that can provide the information they need to make well-informed decisions—ACIDA serves as that agency.

Created in 1970, ACIDA offers eight business expansion and relocation services:

• **workforce analysis**—a detailed analysis of workforce demographics, skills, labor availability and more, according to a company's needs

Community profiling services allow the Armstrong County Industrial Development Authority to promote the amenities of the area that make for a good employee quality of life, such as recreational benefits of nearby Mahoning Creek.

Industrial parks developed by ACIDA, such as Parks Bend Farms, offer prime industrial locations for commercial, service, and light industry business.

• **transportation analysis**—selecting the fastest, most cost-effective routes just about anywhere via air, water, highway, or rail

• **site recommendations**—assistance in selecting a site that meets specified criteria

• **energy/utility services**—data on energy costs, communications services, availability

• **community profiles**—profiles on communities throughout Armstrong County

• **financing assistance**—assistance in locating and applying for various forms of business financing

• **tax facts**—information on tax rates, rebates, and incentives

• **overall coordination**—assistance with a wide range of issues tailored to individual needs.

Through the 1970s and early 1980s, ACIDA served as an underwriter for industrial development bonds. Altogether, it provided financing for 56 companies with more than 4,400 jobs in Armstrong County. In 1987, ACIDA acquired the Kiski Valley Industrial Park.

The next year, ACIDA was designated as the lead agency for economic development by the Armstrong County Board of Commissioners.

Throughout the following decade, ACIDA developed several other industrial parks including the Manor Township Business Park, Parks Bend Farm, West Hills Industrial Park, and Shannock Valley Industrial Center. According to Palilla, these sites offer prime industrial locations for commercial, service, and light industry businesses. Currently in development is a new mixed-use project in South Buffalo Township, to feature light industrial, office, retail, housing, and recreational components. ACIDA also has been instrumental in creating a new small business incubator in Parks Bend Farm that allows entrepreneurs to share overhead costs and support services. ACIDA continues to research and analyze other potential sites for future development.

Through the assistance of ACIDA, more than 11,000 jobs have been added to Armstrong County's economy. In the 1995-97 period alone, more than 700 jobs were created through new businesses. Business expansions accounted for an additional 116 positions. And assistance from ACIDA helped existing businesses to retain 150 more employees.

Harry Carson, Jr., President of Carson Industries, is one of many business leaders who has worked with ACIDA. "A few years ago, we underwent a large expansion, almost doubling the size of our building. ACIDA was very helpful in assisting us with the financing of this project. It would have been tough for us satisfy our needs without them," he said. **Pa**

Merchants Bancorp of Pennsylvania, Inc.
Merchants National Bank of Kittanning

The 1980s and '90s were a time of unprecedented change in the financial services industry. Hundreds of banks and thrifts closed while others were purchased or absorbed into larger banks and non-bank financial institutions. Throughout the country, small town banks became an endangered species. There were some noteworthy exceptions. For example, Merchants National Bank of Kittanning, which celebrated its 100th Anniversary in 1997. Today, as throughout the 20th century, Merchants National Bank remains a pillar of the community where it was chartered back on June 5, 1897.

From the outset, its founders and directors included the cream of Kittanning's commercial, industrial, and legal communities. A judge was elected the bank's first president. Other board members included the president of the local telephone company, the treasurer of the Kittanning Clay Manufacturing Company, a successful clothing merchant, and several other leaders of the business community. They were soon joined by the owners of a nearby woolen mill and a prominent local attorney.

The bank began operations with a capital of $100,000 and established its first business office on the site where the bank remains to this day.

As a convenience to its customers, Merchants National expanded to four locations. In addition to its original Market Street office, a Worthington branch opened in 1967, a branch in West Kittanning opened in 1970, and the newest addition, a Route 422 East branch, opened in 1978. Today, more than 10,000 individual and business customers bank, borrow, save, and meet their credit needs through Merchants National. To accomplish that, the bank maintains assets in excess of $120 million.

Although its primary role has been as a financial institution serving local businesses and residents, Merchants National Bank also supports its community

Merchants National Bank remains a pillar of the Armstrong County community, where it was chartered back on June 5, 1897.

through other channels. For example, in addition to cash contributions to various local charities and nonprofit organizations, the bank's employees, directors and officers share their time and expertise through hundreds of hours of volunteer work. Civic organizations, youth groups, churches, and other worthwhile institutions in Armstrong County have all benefited from involvement by the bank and its people. For Merchants National Bank of Kittanning, the service arena extends well beyond its own walls.

In observance of its 100th anniversary, the bank created a new Armstrong County Community Foundation—and then donated $100,000 to fund it. The Foundation's mission is to make grants to organizations that serve greater Armstrong County in the areas of economic development, health and education, environment, the arts and humanities, historic preservation, and human services.

Dedication to the well-being of its home community is mirrored in

Merchants Bancorp's approach to its customers. In fact, customer service has been prominent throughout its century of service. "We stay close to our customers. We are right here in the heart of the community to serve them," president James R. Drenning points out. As a result, Merchants National Bank today is the largest independent bank in Armstrong County. 🅿

The Worthington Office, the first "branch" bank opened by Merchants, is considered a part of the community.

Beaver County

There are several reasons for Beaver County's rise to prominence as one of the most important industrial powers in the United States. When manufacturing began in the county in the early years of the nineteenth century, the chief reasons were the ready availability of natural resources, the presence of the Ohio and Beaver rivers, and the access those rivers provided to markets hungry for the industrial goods the area produced. Later, as factories grew and manufacturing became more labor intensive, another reason emerged: a large and skilled labor force that worked hard and helped make this the Steel Capital of the World and a dynamic manufacturing center.

The principal reason for this area's decline as an industrial power was the demise of the American steel industry in the 1980s, which led to the closing of the county's huge mills and many of its manufacturing plants that during industry's glory days were the region's principal sources of plentiful and good paying jobs. The downturn cost Beaver County thirty-eight thousand jobs between 1980 and 1987, most of them in steel or steel-related industries, and directly resulted in a dramatic eighteen thousand-person drop in the county's population between 1980 and 1990.

But things are beginning to change. Since the advent of the '90s, Beaver County has begun to make remarkable strides in revitalizing a too-long dormant segment of its economy: manufacturing. Manufacturing employment has risen by about 9 percent since 1990 and now accounts for 19 percent of all the county's jobs. An even more satisfying statistic to people who still remember when steel was king of the industrial hill is this one: some forty-one hundred people now work making steel there, and primary metal manufacturing accounts for 40 percent of all the county's manufacturing jobs.

To the casual observer, those numbers might appear to be a rather modest indicator of economic recovery. They certainly pale in comparison to the employment statistics generated during heavy

The Beaver County River Regatta is a high-speed celebration of the Beaver River, which formed the basis for the development of the county in its earliest days. Photo by Kevin Cooke/Graule Studios

industry's glory days in the county when one company alone, Jones & Laughlin, employed as many as fourteen thousand workers in the biggest steel making complex in southwestern Pennsylvania, one that sprawled for seven miles along the banks of the Ohio River.

But the seemingly modest numbers are noteworthy because they were posted during a time when manufacturing as a percentage of total employment was dropping both statewide and nationwide.

Much of the credit for the success the county has had attracting new manufacturing companies and supporting job growth among companies already operating there goes to elected officials and the economic development professionals. They are the ones who devised the strategies that attracted companies that took over and resumed operations in several of the plants that had been closed and abandoned by the large steel producers

that had been the dominant employer for many years. True, those operations are on a scale significantly smaller than those of the steelmaking giants but they provide meaningful employment to a growing number of people, help create a more healthy economic environment, and give residents reason to be more optimistic about the future.

According to its motto, Beaver County is "Divided By Its Rivers, United By Its People." The people have united behind the economic revitalization effort but they are not mere supporting players. They are a critically valuable and valued

Raccoon State Park draws outdoor enthusiasts for fishing, hiking, and other sports and recreation. Photo by Kevin Cooke/Graule Studios

resource. They are ultimately the lure that attracts new companies to the county and they provide companies already there with good reason to stay and grow.

Economic development people say that the first question they used to be asked by firms considering moving into the county concerned economic incentives. Today, they say, the first questions deal with people, not money. Are enough good people available, they want to know. Can they be trained, they ask.

In Beaver County, the answers increasingly are ones employers want to hear.

The answers reflect some rather impressive demographics. Fully 29 percent of the county's population is in the 25-to-44 age bracket that employers are keenly interested in. Twenty-three percent are under age 18 and are part of a large pool just about to enter their prime learning and job training years. Residents are better educated today, on average, than they were when King Steel reigned. A bigger percentage of those over age 25 are high school and college graduates. More of them are enrolled in college programs than in 1980, many of them at one of the county's four educational institutions—Geneva College in Beaver Falls, Penn State University's Beaver Campus in Monaca, Community College of Beaver County in Monaca, and a Carlow

The biggest employer in Beaver county is the Medical Center of Beaver, with health services constituting the county's largest employment category. Photo by Kevin Cooke/Graule Studios

College facility in Beaver.

These are people who are keenly aware that they live in a new economic environment and must adapt to a new economic culture. They recognize that their best job opportunities locally are not likely to be with huge corporations but with smaller, more agile firms. But they also recognize that the huge corporations that employed their fathers and grandfathers helped forge the county's rich history of industrial achievement that is matched by very few other places in the world.

Beaver County's manufacturing history can be traced to the early days of the nineteenth century in Beaver Falls, named for the Beaver River's waterfalls at that site. The Beaver River, which falls sixty-nine feet in a five-mile stretch, provided the water the early small factories needed to fuel their operations. By 1835, five dams had been built to control the Beaver's flow and eighteen factories lined its banks.

It was on the Ohio River that later and

larger industrial development occurred. There, in 1907, Jones & Laughlin Steel broke ground for its first blast furnace in the county. That single furnace grew eventually into an industrial behemoth that transformed coke, coal, and iron ore into wire, nails, and I-beams. In 1979, on the eve of the catastrophic industrial downturn, the mill produced enough steel to build 100,000 sixty-foot-long bridges.

It was said back then that every steel mill job generated four others in the community. Years ago, steel companies even built some of the communities. Aliquippa, which during steel's glory days grew to have a population of some twenty-seven thousand people, was originally built by Jones & Laughlin Steel as a company town. By the early 1940s, the company was building a new home a day to house employees. J&L not only built the town, it engaged in a bit of social engineering; the company assigned its employees, many of them immigrants from southern and eastern Europe, to live in various neighborhoods according to their ethnic origins.

As predominant as steel was for so many generations, it was not Beaver County's only industrial activity. Early industries included coal mining, lumbering, and boat building, followed later by the manufacturing of glass, tile, brick, ceramics, electric products, roofing, lumber products, chemicals, electrical machinery, and various consumer goods. The county's 1967 Industrial Directory listed 246 firms engaged in such enterprises.

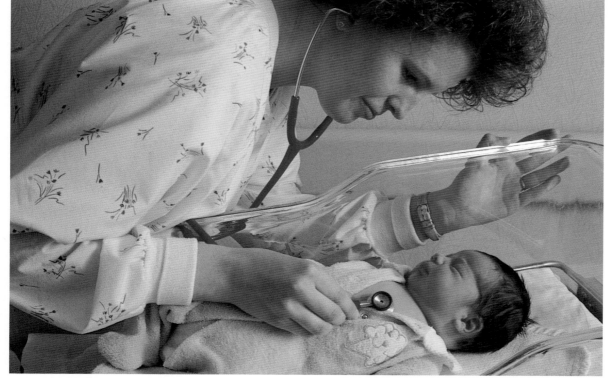

The Brodhead Cultural Center draws people from throughout the area to attend concerts, plays, and special performances in its outdoor amphitheater setting. Photo by Kevin Cooke/Graule Studios

Today, manufacturing is making a steady comeback in Beaver County but more people there work providing services than making things. More than 26 percent of all workers hold jobs in the service sector and the the biggest employer in the county is a service provider, the Medical Center of Beaver. In fact, health services constitute the county's largest employment category, accounting for more than 10 percent of all jobs.

Electric power generation has for years been a large and important industry in the county. The world's first commercially operated atomic power plant, since closed, was located in Shippingport along the Ohio River and Duquesne Light Company, the county's second largest employer, operates both coal-fired and nuclear plants there.

The Ohio and Beaver rivers still play major roles in the county's business recruitment and retention strategies. The rivers are especially important to manufacturing firms that need abundant water

in their operations and many of them rely on waterways as a relatively inexpensive means of transporting goods and raw materials.

Many more rely on roadways. Recent construction projects have greatly improved the county's highway system. The Beaver Valley Expressway provides fast and direct access to the city of Pittsburgh and Pittsburgh International Airport. Indeed, the expressway makes the airport more easily accessible to parts of Beaver County than it is to some areas of Allegheny County, where it is located. And a recently completed portion of Pennsylvania Route 60 is a direct, limited-access road that links the county's center to the Pennsylvania Turnpike and points north.

Airport access makes the Beaver Valley Expressway corridor a prime site for continuing business development. The county-owned Hopewell Industrial Park there, opened in 1987, now is home to many companies that need to be or want to be near the airport.

The private sector also is involved in the job generation effort. There are several privately owned industrial parks in the county located in and around some of the older mills and factories, facilities that in many cases can relatively easily

and quickly be retrofitted to accommodate new manufacturing ventures.

The county's most ambitious—and most long-range—economic development effort involves the development of more than twelve hundred acres of now vacant land along the Ohio River that once was the giant J&L (later LTV) steel mill. Beaver County and a private developer, Bet-Tech International, Inc., bought the land in 1993; the county owns about 120 acres and Bet-Tech owns the rest. The property is being redeveloped as an industrial re-use/brownfield site. A substantial amount of the environmental work at the site already has been done and water and sewer lines have been installed. Both the county and its partner are investing significant amounts of money in the project and are beginning to market it.

Economic development officials say it could take twenty or twenty-five years to redevelop the site that not all that many years ago was the vibrant symbol of the county's economic power. This costly, ambitious undertaking may well transform and revitalize not only a vacant parcel of land but Beaver County's hopes for a more economically secure future as well. **Pa**

Geneva College

Geneva College is a school with a mission. For the past 150 years, it has been steadfast in its pursuit of one goal: to provide young men and women with a quality education built on a strong foundation of Christian teachings and principles.

Today, Geneva College remains grounded in Christian faith and service.

For 150 years, Geneva College has been providing young men and women with a quality education built on a strong Christian foundation. Students can earn undergraduate degrees in more than 40 areas of concentration, as well as pursuing graduate studies.

That approach is reflected in every aspect of its pre-professional curriculum, which combines a diverse selection of liberal arts classes with biblically-based extra-curricular programs.

"We combine our unashamed and distinctive Christian commitment with academic excellence," is the way that Dr. John H. White, the eighteenth president of Geneva, explains it.

In addition to offering traditional fields of study including education, engineering, and business administration, a number of innovative programs such as aviation are also available at Geneva. Students can enroll in studies leading to an associate degree or to a bachelors degree in more than 40 major areas of concentration. For students hoping to continue their studies at the graduate level, Geneva has pre-professional programs in various areas including medicine and law, and the College offers master's degree programs in psychology, higher education, and organizational leadership.

Geneva also provides students with the opportunity to participate in programs offered jointly with other colleges and institutions. These offerings include a unique cooperative work-study program offered through Geneva and the Federal Aviation Administration. Through this program, the FAA trains and certifies selected electrical engineering students in computerized air traffic control.

Founded in 1848 by the Reformed Presbyterian Church of North America, Geneva College was originally established in Northwood, Ohio, directly south of Toledo. However, in 1880, the school relocated to Beaver Falls, Pennsylvania, where it had been awarded a 10-acre land grant from the Harmony Society. Today, the Geneva campus encompasses more than 55 acres in an area that overlooks the Beaver River. The town of Beaver Falls, with a population of 14,000, is approximately 30 miles northwest of Pittsburgh. As a result, Beaver Falls provides Geneva students with a friendly, small-town atmosphere and big-city access.

When the College convened its first session at the Beaver Falls location in 1880, classes had to be held in the nearby Reformed Presbyterian Church building; its academic building on the new campus had not yet been completed. Eight months later, on May 26, 1881, six students—five men and one woman—graduated in the school's first Beaver Falls commencement.

Today, campus enrollment exceeds 1,900 including full- and part-time students in both graduate and undergraduate programs. Residential students come from 20 different states and 28 foreign countries. Approximately 34 percent of the student population at Geneva commutes to class.

Geneva has maintained its accreditation from the Middle States Association of Colleges and Schools ever since 1923. It also holds institutional memberships in a number of other professional organizations and accrediting boards. In addition, the College has repeatedly been recognized by the John M. Templeton Foundation through its Honor Roll for Character-Building Colleges.

Faculty members at Geneva College are evangelical Christians who believe in combining the values of historical Christianity with the school's liberal arts and professional studies curriculum. All full-time faculty hold advanced degrees. More than 80 percent have earned doctorates. The college also makes use of adjunct faculty members with applied backgrounds in industry, arts, and the professions. However, only full-time professors are assigned to serve as academic advisors and counselors. As a result, students and faculty have an opportunity to develop strong relationships.

Inside the classroom, Geneva College maintains a full complement of up-to-date instructional technologies coupled with well-equipped science labs, computer workshops, and library services. The school also offers a variety of services outside the classroom including a Career Development Center, an Office of Multicultural Development, and a variety of student support services as well as an active alumni association.

Of course, life at Geneva College isn't all work. The school's Student Activities Office oversees a wealth of events and organizations including an Aviation Club, Ski Club, Society of Chemistry, and Big Brother and Big Sister programs, to name just a few. The College's radio and television stations offer hands-on experience in communications. Several theatrical events are staged each year. Musicians can try their hand in concert or as members of the marching band. Singers can participate in one of many vocal ensembles or in the chorus known as "The Genevans". Special events such as the "Faith & Law Lecture Series" and

The Geneva campus encompasses more than 55 acres in an area that overlooks the Beaver River.

the "Geneva Lecture and Artist Series" provide cultural as well as spiritual enrichment for students throughout the year.

As a member of both the National Association of Intercollegiate Athletics and the National Christian College Athletic Association, Geneva College offers a well-rounded selection of sports programs. Both men and women participate in intercollegiate as well as intramural teams. The school's involvement in sports is nothing new. Back in 1893, the men's basketball team was recognized as the first college basketball team in U.S. history, making Geneva College the birthplace of college basketball.

Consistent with Geneva College's strong Christian roots, its students enjoy a wide range of opportunities for ministry and Christian outreach. For example, the Senior Citizen ministry, the World Christian Fellowship, and a puppet-based ministry called the Cotton Candy Connection all offer students the chance to act on their religious convictions.

It was precisely this Christian foundation and friendly attitude that convinced Michael Witterman, class of 1998, that Geneva was the college for him. "I knew as soon as I visited Geneva that it was different than other colleges. The people were genuinely interested in me as a person. That made all the difference in the world," he said.

Witterman's observations are right on target in the eyes of College President John White, whose stated goal for Geneva is to sustain its focus on providing Christian-founded education to young men and women. "We would like to become a nationally known, Biblically conservative and academically excellent college," Dr. White said. "Geneva looks forward to the next century." 🅿️

Geneva College campus enrollment exceeds 1,900, including full- and part-time students.

Chapter

4

Butler County

Comparatively low taxes, good schools, a small-town atmosphere, increasing job opportunities, and easy access to Pittsburgh and Pittsburgh International Airport are turning once sleepy, laid-back Butler County into the region's growth dynamo.

Between 1990 and 1996, Butler County's population grew by more than 10 percent—the largest gain of any county in southwestern Pennsylvania. Most of the growth has been in the southwest corner of the county, near its border with Allegheny County. The most dramatic jump has occurred in Seven Fields borough, which has grown by 84 percent. Cranberry Township, which not too long ago was little more than a wide spot on Route 19 most noted for traffic backups caused by vehicles moving between the two interstate highways whose paths cross there—the Pennsylvania Turnpike and Interstate 79—has seen its population swell by about 36 percent. But they aren't the only stars on Butler's growth crown. Overall, forty-three of the county's fifty-seven municipalities recorded population increases since 1990.

Many of the newcomers are from Pittsburgh and its nearby suburbs and they still commute to their jobs in the city and Allegheny County. But a growing number are working closer to their new homes because of new and increasingly more plentiful job opportunities nearby. Manufacturing jobs in the county grew by 2 percent in the most recent twelve-month period, with much of the growth attributed to start-ups and expansions in several industries, notably vinyl products manufacturing, tool and die making, and steel assembly. A manufacturer, Armco Steel, is the county's biggest employer and more than 23 percent of the county's labor force work in manufacturing. That makes manufacturing Butler's largest employment category, according to Pennsylvania Department of Labor and Industry reports.

Most of the new jobs in manufacturing and other segments resulted when established businesses expanded. (To cite an employment rule of thumb: expansion of

Butler County is Pennsylvania's twelfth largest agricultural county. Photo by Kevin Cooke/Graule Studios

established businesses accounts for between 85 percent and 95 percent of all job creation.) But a growing number of Butler's new jobs are being created by business start-ups. From 1992 to 1996, the number of new businesses established there jumped by a very satisfying 10.2 percent.

Equally satisfying is the bottom line of Butler County's employment report. Its unemployment rate of 3.2 percent is the lowest of any county in southwestern Pennsylvania.

Manufacturing traditionally has been an important part of Butler County's economic history. John Roebling, considered to be the greatest American bridge builder of the 19th century, invented the modern steel cable, produced it in his Saxonburg factory, and used it in the many bridges he and his company designed and built.

Steelmakers and other manufacturers have over many years been the county's biggest employers. Early large manufacturing companies included Standard Steel Car Company (later Pullman Standard), a railroad-car manufacturer that was established in the city of Butler, the county seat, in 1902.

Twenty-eight years later, at the onset

of the Great Depression, the city of Butler became a small scale automobile manufacturing center when the American Austin Car Company started producing an auto that was totally different from anything ever built in the country. The American Austin was tiny (1,130 pounds), economical (40 miles to the gallon of gas), inexpensive ($445 f.o.b. Butler), innovative (it likely was the first American-built car with the battery under the hood), and very popular (8,558 were built and sold the first year). But as inexpensive as it was, by 1934 the Austin had become a luxury few could afford and production ceased.

It started again three years later after the American Bantam Car Company bought out American Austin. By 1940 the company turned to producing military equipment. The company made several military products but is best remembered as the designer, developer, and first manufacturer of the legendary Jeep.

Wartime demands soon eclipsed American Bantam's capabilities and Jeep production soon moved to bigger plants

Steelmakers and other manufacturers have over many years been the county's biggest employers. Today, Armco Steel is the county's biggest employer. Photo by Kevin Cooke/Graule Studios

Lake Arthur, located in the 16,000-acre Moraine State Park, has a 40-mile shoreline and is popular for sailing, boating, swimming, and other water sports. Photo by Kevin Cooke/Graule Studios

run by bigger companies. Auto making now is just an interesting footnote in Butler's industrial history. Neither cars nor Jeeps are made in Butler County today but a lot of other things are, including speciality steel, crystals and prisms, fabricated metals, porcelain

Dairy products, animal products, and poultry products make an important contribution to the economy of Butler County. Butler County's more than twelve hundred farms and $54 million plus annual agricultural production make Butler Pennsylvania's twelfth largest agricultural county. Photo by Kevin Cooke/Graule Studios

electrical supplies, tools and dies, copper tubing, foundry equipment, chemicals, cleaning supplies, rubber and plastic products, scientific instruments, medical supplies, stone products, glass and concrete products, machinery, and petroleum products.

Petroleum has been on the product list for years. Before Butler County became a manufacturing power, it was a major oil industry player. During America's first oil boom of the 1870s and '80s, there were more than a thousand producing oil wells in the county. In 1872 a wildcat well was brought in that allowed the town of Petrolia to proclaim itself "oil capital of the world." Before that, Petrolia had three houses; afterward it had four hotels, twelve grocery stores, two hardware stores, seven barber shops, a newsroom, three doctors, several lawyers and at least one saloon for every business in town. Petrolia's population peaked at five thousand before the boom went bust. Today, its population is about three hundred.

Wildcatters were drilling for oil when they discovered the county's first major gas well near Fairview in 1872. And the nation's first pipeline built to carry natural gas for manufacturing purposes linked a well in Clinton Township to a factory in Etna in Allegheny County. There still are many productive, paying wells in the county and natural gas continues to make a meaningful contribution to the Butler's economy.

So does agriculture. Butler has been called the Buckwheat County since 1859, when a severe late frost killed corn and wheat crops. County farmers, desperate to salvage their livelihoods, reworked their fields and planted buckwheat. The crop was immediately successful. At one time, the numerous water-powered mills on the banks of the county's many streams were famous for their skill in processing buckwheat into flour. Today two mills in Prospect and West Sunbury still do the job.

Industrial, commercial, residential, and infrastructure development have cut agriculture acreage in the county. And agriculture today provides employment for less than 1 percent of the county's labor force. Still, however, its more than twelve hundred farms and $54-million-plus annual agricultural production make Butler Pennsylvania's twelfth largest agricultural county.

Horticultural specialties (greenhouse

and nursery products, seeds, and landscaping) and mushrooms are the biggest crops and bring in $24.4 million a year. They are followed by dairy products, animal products, field crops (corn, hay, wheat, oats, soybeans), vegetables, potatoes, fruit, and poultry products.

While agriculture and mining are in decline in the county, service businesses and retailing are thriving there. So is health care, which accounts for almost half of all the county's service-sector jobs.

Recreation is not one of Butler's big job generators but it is important nonetheless because recreational opportunities attract people—from both inside and outside the county—with time and dollars to spend. The county's biggest recreation complex is 16,000-acre Moraine State Park. The park's Lake Arthur has 40-mile shoreline and is popular for swimming, boating, sailing, ice skating, and ice fishing. There is a 400-acre lake at the county's Glades Waterfowl Area, which is open for public fishing and hunting. There are three state gamelands totaling about 9,360 acres located in the county. Three private country clubs, sixteen commercial golf courses, and numerous county and municipal parks add to the recreation picture.

Abundant recreational facilities are a

Horticultural specialites including greenhouse and nursery products are Butler County's biggest crops. Photo by Kevin Cooke/Graule Studios

real plus for the county. Besides attracting visitors, they are high on the list of amenities of people and businesses looking to relocate. They are, therefore, an important part of the county's all important economic development effort.

The county's job-producing, people- and business-attracting record in recent years shows that effort to be on the right track. And if the recent past has been bright and promising, so is the immediate future.

To accommodate anticipated future growth opportunities, economic development leaders in the county are focusing on establishing new business and industrial parks. There are presently four business parks in various stages of development in the area and a fifth park along Interstate 79 in Jackson Township is completely filled. Next up: development of a 426-acre site in Saxonburg that was a USX sintering plant. Under serious discussion are plans to locate parks in several other areas of the county.

Butler government and economic development officials are working on a number of programs to expand the business and industrial park system and implement other economic development initiatives. And they, along with their colleagues from other counties in the region, are lobbying hard for a number of road construction and improvement projects to modernize the county's highway network. The other counties are involved because the road projects, especially those planned for areas north of the city of Butler where the highway system is considered to be inadequate to support aggressive economic growth efforts, will ultimately benefit the entire Pittsburgh region.

The Kaufman House, a local restaurant, is a favorite gathering place for county residents, and a pleasant discovery for visitors. Photo by Kevin Cooke/Graule Studios

Butler County sees new business start-ups as vital for long-term new job growth. To encourage such activity, economic development leaders and the Butler County Community College have put together a program showing budding entrepreneurs how to start a business, write a business plan, arrange financing, and take care of other business essentials.

According to a recent industry study, Butler County before the '90s end should experience the biggest growth in manufacturing jobs of any of Pennsylvania's top twenty-five industrial areas. County officials recognize that growth of that magnitude has to be planned for so that it does not overwhelm an already fast-paced economic environment. So they can properly and realistically handle future growth, not only in manufacturing but in all segments of the county's economy, they are developing a county strategic plan that will include segments on land development, transportation, education, and agriculture. They see the plan's development and implementation as an exercise in avoidance: it will enable them to avoid the kind of unplanned, careless, and haphazard growth that has slowed and even sunk burgeoning economic recovery efforts in some other places. **Pa**

Butler Memorial Hospital

When is a hospital not a hospital? When it is the acute care component of a comprehensive service group known as a health care system.

In the hundred years since Butler Memorial Hospital was created by its community, the concept of health and healing has undergone radical change. And Butler Memorial Hospital—today the hub of an extensive Butler Health System—has been there at every step.

From the day it opened its twenty-bed facility in 1898, Butler Memorial Hospital has helped people recover from illness and injury.

As demand grew for its healing services, Butler Hospital administrators and employees realized that a relocation from their original confined site would be required. Just twenty-four years after its creation, a new Butler Memorial Hospital opened with 194 patient beds.

The 1970s marked an exciting new era of tremendous growth in medical tech-

Butler Memorial Hospital has served Butler County and the surrounding community for more than 100 years, always growing to meet the needs of the people who live here.

nology and unprecedented expansion of hospital-based treatment programs. Nuclear medicine, intensive care, and coronary care all came into play at Butler Memorial during the early 1970s.

In the 1980s, with its new Main Wing now offering extra space, that expansion of services continued. Programs and facilities dealing with substance abuse, angiography, neurosurgery, and laser surgery were all introduced. But perhaps more important—because they foreshadowed the hospital's ultimate transformation into an element of Butler Health System—were the addition of outpatient, satellite, and preventive services.

A 1985 Urgent Care Center in fast-growing Cranberry Township was the hospital's first such community outreach project, a service that has now grown into a primary care physician site and an advanced physical rehab facility, outpatient drug and alcohol services, and specialty physicians' offices.

Three years later, the cardiac rehabilitation program opened at the hospital, offering education and exercise for those recovering from heart attacks and heart surgery.

Soon after, a mobile MRI and a Breast Imaging Center became available. So did primary care physician services at five separate locations. The Butler Memorial Hospital Heart Center was added in 1998 to combat heart

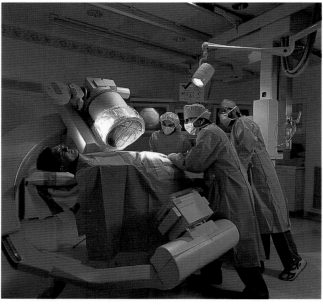

Throughout the years, Butler Memorial Hospital has been on the forefront of technological advances in medicine, offering the latest in angiography, neurosurgery, and laser surgery among its hospital-based programs.

disease by offering cardiac surgery procedures on site. As each new service opened, the role of Butler Memorial Hospital itself continued to change. No longer was the hospital there to treat just the sick. In its new form, at the dawn of the information age, the hospital's role had expanded into helping healthy people stay healthy.

Getting people home and out of the hospital rather than in house for lengthy treatment and convalescence became hallmarks of Butler Memorial.

Today, 70 percent of the hospital's surgeries are provided on an outpatient basis. A nationally recognized community health planning process, involving providers throughout the county, continues to identify community health care needs and new approaches to treating them. And programming to prevent illness and injury, as well as acute care to treat them, has become the foundation for the new age of health care anchored by Butler Memorial Hospital. ◧

Chapter

5

Fayette County

On average today, it takes people living in Fayette County only twenty-one minutes to travel to their jobs. About seven out of every ten of those commuters work within the county's borders and more than half of them have jobs in retailing and with companies providing some form of service.

As enviable as that short commute may appear to those who live in more heavily populated and traffic-congested areas of the region, there are those Fayette Countians who do not consider it an unmixed blessing. They say the reason so many residents work so close to home is that it is not very easy for many of them to get to jobs farther away, both inside and outside the county. But there are forces at work to change that.

Fayette's government, civic, and business leaders have fought long and hard for transportation improvement projects that are needed to give residents easier, faster access to jobs both within and outside the county's borders, and to provide county businesses with more direct and faster access to customers and suppliers. They point out that Pittsburgh and the international airport are not that many miles away as the crow flies, but it is an arduously meandering trip if the crow must travel by highway.

So they have to be pleased with the progress being made on the Mon-Fayette Expressway. The southern part of the expressway linking Pittsburgh and West Virginia runs pretty much along the Monongahela River, which forms Fayette's western border. Under discussion for almost thirty years, the road is a key element of the economic development and revitalization plans of Fayette, Greene, and Washington counties and the southeastern sector of Allegheny County. Building the road is an enormous undertaking with an enormous price tag: it is

A statue of the Marquis de la Fayette stands watch outside the elegant Nemacolin Woodlands Resort and Spa in Fayette County. Photo courtesy of the Nemacolin Woodlands Resort and Spa

the most expensive highway construction project in Pennsylvania history.

The expressway will serve to complement the county's current major highway, U.S. Route 119, which affords

The Ohiopyle State Park offers white-water rafting adventure on the Ohiopyle River. Photo by Kevin Cooke/Graule Studios

Fayette a direct link with Interstate 76, the Pennsylvania Turnpike.

The Mon-Fayette Expressway likely will be as critical to the county's economic future as the National Road was to the development of commerce there in the early 1800s. That road from Wheeling, West Virginia, to Cumberland, Maryland, now U.S. Route 40, ran right up Main Street in Uniontown, the county seat. It was the very first federally supported roadway in the country and was the nation's busiest land artery to the west. (The road's routing may have been influenced by Albert Gallatin, entrepreneur, politician, diplomat, financier, scholar, and a major influence in the shaping of the early republic, who lived near New Geneva. He served as Secretary of the Treasury and was instrumental in financing not only the National Road but also the Louisiana Purchase and the Lewis and Clark Expedition.)

Before the National Road was built, the Monongahela and Youghiogheny rivers were the area's key links to the outside world. The Mon made transportation of coal possible and the Yough was a very important commercial waterway. Flatboats built in Connellsville transported the area's principal products to market: salt, pig metal, hollow ironware, whiskey (remember the Whiskey Rebellion), and flour.

And just as the National Road supplanted the rivers as the county's main transportation link in the early 1800s, a railroad line from Connellsville to Pittsburgh that opened in 1860 took away much of the travel commerce from the National Road.

The area was flexing its industrial muscles long before the railroad arrived and even prior to Fayette County's establishment in September 1783 on a 794-square-mile tract of land taken from Westmoreland County. Indeed, the county and the republic itself were still in their infancy (the first battle of the French and Indian War, which determined which of the world powers would colonize the New World, was fought at Fort Necessity near Uniontown only a few decades earlier) when the first glass factory west of Allegheny Mountains was established in New Geneva in 1794. The world's first mill to puddle and roll iron began operating in 1817 at a site between Connellsville and Brownsville. And the world's first cast iron bridge was erected over Dunlap's Creek in Brownsville in 1835.

Other notable Fayette firsts: the first bank west of the Alleghenies was established in 1814 in Perryopolis; in 1827 a small college in Uniontown whose name has been erased from history's pages was the first institution of higher learning in the United States to offer a course in

Winter offers opportunities for those who enjoy skiing to take to the slopes nearby, including the Sundial Ski Lodge, which offers skiing and snowboarding opportunities for people of all abilities, and a Ski Academy. Photo courtesy of the Nemacolin Woodlands Resort and Spa

agriculture; and the machine gun was invented by Isaac Newton Lewis of Uniontown. Less notable, perhaps, but noteworthy nonetheless: McDonald's Big Mac sandwich was invented by James Delligatti, a franchisee in Uniontown.

The area was an early center of the coal and coke industry. The coal seam running through the Connellsville Basin held the world's finest coking coal for making steel. The first beehive oven in the United States was designed and built in Connellsville in 1833, and the world's largest single bank of coke ovens once operated in Perryopolis along present state Route 51.

Upon its discovery, coal became more than an industry in the county, it was a preoccupation bordering on obsession. Virtually all other commercial activity was suspended while landowners and cagey entrepreneurs engaged in a frenzied buying and selling of coal tracts. For a while more attention was paid to—and more money was made from—the buying and selling of coal land than the actual mining of coal. Thanks to land sales and coal-related activities, Uniontown became a financial center rivaling steelmakers Pittsburgh and Johnstown and was said to have had more millionaires

per capita than any town in the United States.

Coal no longer is a millionaire maker in Fayette and mining does not provide many job opportunities. But glass still is an important local industry and manufacturing—of glass products and other commodities—is the county's third largest employment category after retailing and service.

More job opportunities in manufacturing and other categories are opening up in the county, thanks largely to organized economic development efforts begun in earnest in 1991 when the Fay-Penn Economic Development Council was established. The Council, working with the county commissioners, the Fayette Industrial Fund, other agencies and municipalities from throughout the county, and business and civic organizations, has an impressive list of accomplishments.

The joint efforts have attracted three new major employers to Fayette (and undoubtedly a number of smaller ones) and convinced at least one major established company to keep its operations and its jobs in the county. Since 1992, more than ninety economic development projects have been completed, almost thirty-three hundred jobs have been either created or retained, more than $34.6 million has been added to the county's annual payroll, and more than $1.6 million in new taxes have been generated on an annual basis. About $70 million has been invested in new projects, most

of it (about 73 percent) private money, and more than $18 million has been spent on new construction.

Three industrial parks owned by non-profit groups—Fayette Industrial Fund, Connellsville Industrial Enterprises, and the Fayette County Redevelopment Authority—now operate in the county and a fourth is in development. There is one privately owned park in operation. The Fay-Penn Industrial Development Council and the Fayette Industrial Fund recently completed a more-than $1.2 million, two-year-long infrastructure development project at the Fayette Business Park in Georges Township.

And in an effort to ensure that many of Fayette's industries and businesses continue to have access to rail service, Fay-Penn, with financial help from the Pennsylvania Department of Transportation, in 1996 acquired and has rehabilitated almost twenty-five miles of rail line. The line now is part of a 65-mile-long system called the Southwest Pennsylvania Railroad, which provides businesses in both Fayette and Westmoreland counties with access to large rail carriers and the markets they serve.

When they list the county's most important assets, the resources available to employers looking for a good place to locate or expand, leaders cite low cost, developable sites and the availability of a trained and trainable, motivated labor force eager to contribute to the revitalization of Fayette's economy. And the county has taken significant steps to increase the value its people asset by working to expand job training opportunities. Fay-Penn has developed programs that match training to the specific needs of local businesses, and specialists in work force development are helping businesses get job-training funds and provide technical assistance on work force related activities.

Fayette County's economic revitalization strategies are showing positive results. The challenge now, leaders admit, is to keep the momentum rolling so they have developed a countywide strategic plan. Called Fayette Forward, it is an all encompassing revitalization blueprint and is considered by many to be one of the most comprehensive of its type in United States. First published in 1995 with 153 projects in areas of business and education, tourism, infrastructure, economic development, marketing, and social conditions, it has since grown to contain 237 projects and has added a seventh area: agriculture. Fifty projects already have been implemented and 260 organizations have been recruited to par-

Fallingwater is a cantilevered architectural masterpiece designed by Frank Lloyd Wright and located in the scenic hills of the Laurel Highlands. The home is considered to be one of the most famous homes in the country. Photo courtesy Laurel Highlands Visitors Bureau

ticipate. During any given week, anywhere from 500 to 1,000 volunteers from those organizations can be working on the various projects.

They work anonymously for the most part but no less diligently and with the same spirit—if not on as grand a scale—that motivated one of Fayette County's most illustrious native sons, George Catlett Marshall. Born and raised in Uniontown, Marshall was an army general, secretary of state, and secretary of defense. He is most noted for being the author of the Marshall Plan that helped a devastated Europe recover after World War II and for which he was awarded the Nobel Peace Prize in 1953.

Fort Necessity National Battlefield is the site of George Washington's first battle and only loss. Photo courtesy Laurel Highlands Visitors Bureau

His generosity, unselfishness, and diligence in pursuing goals that many thought unattainable can serve today to motivate and inspire those who are working to return Fayette County to its accustomed prominent position of prominence in southwest Pennsylvania. 𝐏𝐚

Chapter

6

Golden Triangle:
The City of Pittsburgh

D on't call it the Smoky City. Smoke from steel mills, foundries, and railroads gave Pittsburgh that nickname (and a few others even more unflattering) during the 1930s, '40s, and early '50s. That's when steel was king in Pittsburgh and steel making was a dirty job, when the smoke and dirt made living and working almost anywhere in the city as unhealthy as it was unpleasant. But dirt and smoke-filled skies meant prosperity in a place that had experienced plenty of both almost from its founding in 1758, and being called the Smoky City was considered a badge of honor.

Smoke control legislation by the City Council fifty years ago began to change all that. The laws, along with more efficient pollution-control technologies, allowed Pittsburgh's civic and business leaders to launch a massive cleanup effort in the 1950s that transformed the city's drab, dingy, dirty downtown into a bright, clean, and pleasant place. Pittsburgh gladly surrendered its Smoky City nickname and adopted a new one, America's Renaissance City.

But even America's Renaissance City could not realistically rid itself of all its industrial smoke and dirt, not when its mills and factories continued to boom through 1960s, and '70s. Pittsburgh did not achieve virtual smoke-free status until the early 1980s—the result not of legislation or improved technology but of the virtual demise of the area's steel industry. The closing of the mills also cost Pittsburgh and the region their claim to another nickname, Steel Capital of the World.

Since then, Pittsburgh and the region have actively and at times frantically pursued one or more

In addition to being a center point for business, industry, research, and education, Pittsburgh is home to three rivers—the Allegheny, Monongahela, and Ohio—and three professional sports franchises—the Pittsburgh Pirates baseball team, Pittsburgh Steelers football team, and Pittsburgh Penguins hockey team. Photo by Kevin Cooke/Graule Studios

replacements for steel as their economic foundation. The pursuit has been complicated by the fact that almost every other metropolitan center in the country is on a similar quest.

But despite some setbacks and a few false starts, considerable progress has been made and the City of Pittsburgh remains the region's business, financial, medical, research, educational, and cultural hub. And although the city may be losing population, to not only its suburbs

but to exurbs in nearby counties as well, many former residents still return every day to work, to study at the eight colleges and universities located within its borders (Carlow, Carnegie-Mellon, Chatham, Community College of Allegheny County, Duquesne, Point Park, Robert Morris, and the University of Pittsburgh,) or to attend classes at the city's numerous vocational and trade schools.

Long before the mills closed, Pittsburgh actively sought to diversify its economy. When the ax fell and thousands of steelworkers and others were sent trooping to the unemployment office, the search intensified and Pittsburgh set out to make a high-tech name for itself. Fortunately, there was an established base in place that could be built upon: medical and industrial research.

When Pittsburgh was the center of one of the most prolifically industrialized areas in the world it was the headquarters city for many of the country's leading industrial companies. Those companies operated extensive research facilities throughout the area and employed a small army of the best research scientists in their fields. And the city long has been an outstanding medical research center. Probably the defining moment in Pittsburgh's rise to a position of world leadership in medical research came in the mid-1950s when Dr. Jonas Salk, a University of Pittsburgh researcher, developed the first successful anti-polio vaccine. In more recent years, the city has become noted and respected as a center for organ transplantation.

The annual Three Rivers Regatta event, a four-day festival featuring boat racing, a water-bound parade, airshow, outdoor concert and fireworks, is highlighted with a hot-air balloon launch. Photo by Kevin Cooke/Graule Studios

Using medical and industrial research as a foundation—or, at least, a model—Pittsburgh for most of the past two decades has vigorously pursued a high-tech future. And while one would hardly confuse Pittsburgh with Silicon Valley, great strides have been made. The city has achieved considerable high-tech success, thanks in large measure to such resources as Carnegie-Mellon University's Robotics Institute and Software Institute, and the University of Pittsburgh's exceptional research capabilities.

CMU and its Oakland neighbor, Pitt, both highly regarded research universities, have been longtime rivals for research dollars and recognition, but there is evidence of late of more cooperation between them. They have for years jointly operated the Pittsburgh Supercomputer Center in suburban Monroeville, and CMU reportedly is pursuing Pitt as a partner in a major research and teaching effort in biotechnology that would link its computer and information technology expertise to Pitt's highly regarded medical research capabilities.

Besides helping put themselves and the city into the high-tech research spotlight, the two schools have generated some significant economic benefits as well. For example, CMU's office of technology transfer, which is involved with licensing and commercializing university-developed technologies, has filed more than fifty patents and signed about that same number of licensing agreements, which have brought in more than $40 million since 1993. CMU officials say that more than seventy technology-based companies have ties with the school.

Most of the region's 170 research facilities and almost all of its 700 biomedical, biotechnology, and life science companies are headquartered in the city—many of them clustered near the Pitt and CMU

Pittsburgh is an intriguing blend of historic and modern architecture. Photo by Kevin Cooke/Graule Studios

campuses. And many, if not most, of the 450 software firms that have been established in the region in recent years are headquartered in the city.

In the wake of a slowly recovering service- and technology-based economy, Pittsburgh is undergoing its third renaissance. While not as overwhelmingly transforming as the fabled first one in the 1950s nor as ambitious as the second in the '80s (which added new major office buildings to the downtown skyline), the latest effort nevertheless is a sign of renewed vigor, commitment, and confidence.

This smaller scale renaissance began with a boom. That was the sound made when what long ago had been the city's tallest building was imploded in May 1997 to make way for a new department store—the first freestanding department store to be built in the United States in more than a decade, according to development officials.

The $78 million department store project has spawned a proposal to reinvigorate the city's main downtown shopping corridor along Fifth and Forbes avenues. Under the so-called Downtown Retail/Entertainment Project, estimated to cost $178 million, the city and a private developer will jointly acquire properties along both streets and lease or sell them to national retailers and entertainment companies. It would be the largest downtown development project since Renaissance II.

The most costly current undertaking— totaling about $800 million—is a three-pronged project to: (1) expand the undersized David L. Lawrence Convention Center, downtown, nearly tripling its exhibition space and adding meeting rooms and a ballroom; (2) build a 38,000-seat baseball park for the Pittsburgh Pirates; and (3) build a 66,000-seat football stadium for the Pittsburgh Steelers. Three Rivers Stadium on the North Side will be demolished and additional nearby property is being acquired to make

room for the new ball fields.

Pittsburgh's two largest locally headquartered banks, PNC and Mellon, are building huge operations centers downtown, each costing $100 million or more. The projects not only will help solidify the city's role as one of the country's leading financial centers, they also put to productive use parcels of long underused but extremely valuable downtown land.

Alcoa, the Aluminum Company of America, is spending an estimated $47 million to build a new headquarters complex on the North Side.

The elaborate domes of the Immaculate Heart of Mary cathedral are striking in their architectural detail. Photo by Kevin Cooke/Graule Studios

Also underway or in the active planning stage in the city:
• Construction of an $8 million, two-tiered riverside park along the south bank of the Allegheny River from the Point, where the Allegheny and Monongahela rivers join to form the Ohio, to the convention center.
• A new $18 million downtown building to house the Pittsburgh Public Theater.

The theater is the latest undertaking of the Pittsburgh Cultural Trust, a non-profit organization established to develop a cultural district downtown and encourage the arts in the region.
• The $42 million Federal-North Redevelopment project to revitalize a largely blighted North Side neighborhood.
• The Village At Washington's Landing, a townhouse/office/ light manufacturing complex by a private developer nearing completion on Herr's Island in the Allegheny River that once housed slaughterhouses.
• A planned $300 million project to build a residential/office/retail complex on a 130-acre site on the South Side where the city's largest steel making complex once stood. (As many as six thousand jobs could be created with the project, city officials say.)
• The Heights of South Hills, a plan by a private developer to build 1,100 single family homes, townhouses, and apartments on a 672-acre tract on the South Side Slopes.
• A 1,000-home development in the East End on a hill created over many years with slag from nearby steel mills dumped there.
• A $30 million project to nearly quadruple the size of the renowned Phipps Conservatory in Schenley Park in Oakland and add botanical gardens that city officials say would be the finest in the United States.
• The construction, costing approximately $60 million, of a convocation center/basketball arena on the University of Pittsburgh's Oakland campus.

And all that, city officials are eager to say, is just the beginning. As renaissances go, they insist, you ain't seen nothin' yet. They are intent on building on the accomplishments of the past four years when, according to Mayor Tom Murphy, $837 million was invested in city development projects and 7,300 jobs were created or retained.

To move developments along further and faster, the city and Allegheny County have combined their economic development offices, which often have competed with each other to attract new businesses and new jobs.

That combined office is scheduled to move into a 31-story building that was Alcoa's downtown headquarters—and the world's first aluminum-clad office building. Alcoa has donated the building to a division of the Southwestern Pennsylvania Regional Planning Commission to be the central office for the region's economic development agencies.

Gathering all the counties' agencies under one roof should, observers say, make them more effective and improve cooperation. And that would make attracting new companies and new jobs to the city and the region a whole lot easier. **Pa**

Renovations in and around downtown Pittsburgh have made it a warm and friendly location for businesses and shoppers. Photo by Kevin Cooke/Graule Studios

(below) Pittsburgh is poised on the brink of a new century, and ready to grow into the future. Photo by Kevin Cooke/Graule Studios

The Carnegie Science Center, named for philanthropist Andrew Carnegie, whose influence can be felt throughout Pittsburgh and the region, has been dubbed "an amusement park for the mind." It houses four floors of displays where children and adults can learn about science and the environment through a variety of interactive exhibits. Photo by Kevin Cooke/Graule Studios

(above, left) Pittsburgh is home to the National Aviary, where a wide variety of rare and endangered birds are housed for education and conservation programs. Photo by Kevin Cooke/Graule Studios

(above, right) Many Pittsburgh communities retain the architecture and flavor of their heritage, such as the community of Polish Hill. Photo by Kevin Cooke/Graule Studios

ALLIANCE National Incorporated
(Formerly HQ Business Centers)

An Atlanta-based software firm, a recent startup, wishes to expand operations to the Pittsburgh metropolitan area. The firm decides to set up its first office in Foster Plaza to retain the advantages of a suburban lifestyle while maintaining easy access to downtown. The firm seeks the easiest, most cost-effective way to enter the new market.

A self-employed estate and business planning professional works out of his home, but several hours a week he needs to use a fully staffed and equipped upscale office to meet with clients.

One of the largest financial institutions in the country is rolling out a nationwide network of 72 locations—including locations in Pittsburgh, Chicago, Cleveland, Columbus, Boston, and Washington, DC—that will provide investment and other financial services. The corporation seeks to have each office up and running within 48 hours of signing the lease.

A growing Los Angeles-based advertising agency seeks to establish an office in downtown Pittsburgh to provide better service to its clients. The firm wants to minimize its investment in support staff and infrastructure without cutting corners in meeting the needs of its clients.

Businesses like these and many others have found the solution to their needs at ALLIANCE NATIONAL Incorporated,

Fully equipped conference rooms are the perfect setting to meet with business associates.

which operates ALLIANCE Business Centers in the Pittsburgh metropolitan area.

Like other top executive suite companies, ALLIANCE provides clients with fully staffed, furnished, and equipped offices with flexible leases in premier locations. Businesses can open a complete office operation with a short-term lease in just 24 hours for less than the cost of hiring a receptionist.

"We provide a complete, work-ready environment that is comparable to that of the executive offices of top corporations," explained David Beale, ALLIANCE's founder, president, and CEO. "Then we manage everything in that setting, so that our clients don't have to worry about day-to-day operations. This frees them to build their businesses, which is far and away their greatest need."

As a successful young entrepreneur, not long out of college, David Beale invested in his first executive suite in 1987. At first it was a casual decision, but then it became a lifelong commitment.

Beale had seen many companies, especially startups, invest precious time and

capital in finding, furnishing, equipping, staffing, and managing facilities instead of using these scarce resources to conduct business. For some, these costs had proved fatal.

The executive suite, he believed, offered a much better way. Small businesses, entrepreneurs, and startups could use the facilities to build their businesses and then move to traditional quarters if and when the time was right. Larger companies that wished to enter new markets could test the waters and develop realistic strategic plans before investing in conventional space and overhead.

As he came to see it, the executive suite could change the way people did business. Today there is much talk of the virtual office, telecommuting, and hoteling, but the executive suite was the first "alternative officing strategy" and it is still the most popular.

Dedicated to the concept, Beale built his business, lease by lease, facility by facility, focusing his efforts in the Northeast, particularly New York and Washington, DC. To meet the needs of

Courteous receptionists greet your visitors in our well-appointed reception areas.

major corporations, he co-founded the ALLIANCE Business Centers NETWORK—an organization of top-quality regional operators who provide reciprocal services to each other's clients as well as a national accounts program for clients who need to enter markets across the country. Today, the NET-WORK links 250 centers in the United States and 21 other countries.

As ALLIANCE grew, the executive suite industry continued to be dominated by mom-and-pop firms. Small firms—even joined together in the NET-WORK—could not fulfill the potential of the executive suite concept and meet the needs of the new companies and industries the rapidly evolving information-based, technology-driven economy of the 90s was creating.

It was inevitable, Beale reasoned, that the industry would consolidate and a couple of leaders would emerge as the dominant players. If he were to prosper in the industry he believed in so strongly, he would need to become the leader.

In 1996 he lined up financing and began the most ambitious expansion plan the industry had yet seen. In less than two years, he expanded his business from 14 facilities in a few Northeastern markets to 75 facilities in

A professional support staff is constantly on hand to provide administrative, word processing, and desktop publishing services.

24 markets nationwide. Plans call for this number to be doubled within a year.

ALLIANCE entered the Pittsburgh market in a dramatic way in March of 1998 when Beale acquired HQ Business Centers of Pittsburgh, Cleveland, and Columbus with nine facilities including three business centers in the Pittsburgh market, at Foster Plaza, One Oxford Centre, and 300 Oxford Drive.

"It's an important, resilient region with a strong technological and industrial base," Beale explained. "Our clients who want to do business in Pittsburgh expect us to be there to serve them."

The acquisition had been one of HQ's leading franchisee groups and HQ Business Centers was the largest and most well-known organization in the business. For observers of the executive suite industry, it was a big development—sort of like Diamler-Benz buying Chrysler.

"We feel incredibly fortunate to have reached an agreement with HQ Business Centers of Pittsburgh, Cleveland, and Columbus," Beale said. "The company has been exceedingly well managed with a high-quality staff and strategically located facilities. For 14 years it has been a premier franchise group in the HQ organization."

Before accepting ALLIANCE's offer, Calvin W. Hunter, HQ's CEO, flew to New York. "Normally, you expect the buyer to visit the seller," he said. "But we went the other way. I flew to New York to satisfy myself about ALLIANCE as a buyer to get a feel for their culture, to meet

Videoconferencing at Foster Plaza is a cost-effective alternative to long-distance meetings.

some of their people, to understand the benefits they'd offer my employees and clients. Before I accepted the ALLIANCE offer, I needed to be sure they'd be taken care of."

"The fact that HQ was a top firm was critical to our strategy," said Beale. "We will keep all management in place. Former employees of HQ will enjoy the same training, development, and participation programs as all ALLIANCE managers and associates. Clients will continue to enjoy the top-notch support and services HQ provided as well as the newly developed programs ALLIANCE has pioneered in technology, marketing, and relocation.

"Our goal is to create a national brand as familiar and dependable as Federal Express or Marriott," Beale explained. ▣

BridgeStreet Accommodations

Family relocation can be stressful and disorienting. So can business travel. BridgeStreet Accommodations—one of America's premier specialty housing firms—was created with a single mission in mind: to make life easier for business travelers and for their relocating families. In the Pittsburgh area alone, BridgeStreet offers more than 300 one-, two-, and three-bedroom apartments which accommodate guests in nine different locations.

Formerly known in Pittsburgh as Temporary Corporate Housing and Corporate Lodgings, BridgeStreet Accommodations now serves the area with apartments in the heart of downtown Pittsburgh, North Hills, western suburbs, South Hills, and in Pittsburgh's fashionable east area. However, Pittsburgh isn't the only place that BridgeStreet makes travelers feel right at home. The company offers accommodation services in cities throughout the United States, Canada, and London.

BridgeStreet Accommodations was formed in the fall of 1997, when five leading providers of temporary housing joined forces. The resulting international organization offers a variety of housing options in a growing number of business centers around the world. BridgeStreet

continues to scout new locations for expansion to meet the steadily increasing global needs of its clients and guests.

BridgeStreet provides full-size, fully equipped apartments, in established residential buildings, located in real-life neighborhoods. Unlike cramped hotel suites, BridgeStreet Accommodations allow guests to feel comfortable and at home in spacious living quarters. "Our apartments have full-sized kitchens, bathrooms, bedrooms, dining areas, and living rooms," Patti Joyce, general manager of BridgeStreet's Pittsburgh branch, points out. Each location is convenient to shopping, recreational sites, athletic facilities, and schools, as well as major business centers and the Pittsburgh International Airport.

For the busy business traveler or for relocating families, BridgeStreet provides lodgings for stays as brief or as lengthy as needed. Guests can stay from as little as one evening to as much as several months or even longer. Advance travel planning requirements are kept to a minimum. No leases or security deposits are required. And guests

BridgeStreet offers full-size, fully equipped apartments, in established residential buildings, located in real-life neighborhoods. It's a more home-like alternative to the usual temporary housing choices.

can pack light; the fully-furnished apartments come stocked with all of the necessities. Linens, towels, cookware, utensils, dishes, coffeemakers, microwaves, washers, dryers, irons, cable television, and even a corkscrew are all provided. Several BridgeStreet locations also offer such optional services as baby-sitting, grocery or restaurant delivery, and dry cleaning.

BridgeStreet is unique in the U.S. temporary housing industry in that it economically satisfies overnight accommodation needs with Monday-through-Friday housekeeping services for short-term guests, according to Ms. Joyce. For guests staying 30 days or longer, staff housekeepers provide weekly services. Should unexpected repairs and maintenance requirements arise, they are also handled quickly and professionally.

Rates at BridgeStreet Accommodations vary according to location, length of stay,

Residents in a BridgeStreet Accommodations apartment will find all the amenities in their fully stocked apartment: linens, towels, cookware, utensils, dishes, coffeemakers, microwave ovens, and more are provided.

and apartment features. But they are calculated to provide consistent value to the company's customers. As a result, BridgeStreet's prices compare favorably with those of commercial hotels serving the same cities. As an added convenience to customers, the company uses a single-invoice billing system with payment cycles tailored to each client. Pre-billing is also available so that business guests can be reimbursed quickly for travel and accommodation expenses through their employers. A central, toll-free BridgeStreet phone line helps to make reservations easy from any location.

BridgeStreet Accommodations works closely with many companies whose business travel includes consultants, professionals in training, or short-term work assignments. Universities, medical centers, training organizations, and the performing arts are among the company's growing assortment of clients. Typical guests might include families relocating, actors with touring companies, and professionals in need of lodgings for a week-long seminar.

Whether it's a family waiting for their new home to be finished or someone looking for extra space to house visiting relatives—BridgeStreet can help. "Everyone can use our services," according to Ms. Joyce.

Whatever the need and whoever the client, BridgeStreet housing specialists assist their customers in finding the best accommodations at the right rates. During 1997, that amounted to nearly 10,000 reservations. Customer service is part of the reason. In every BridgeStreet city, guests are provided with a comprehensive directory of services. These directories contain information about local services, schools, stores, and regional products as well as a wealth of other important information. Even more important, BridgeStreet staff members are on call 24 hours a day, seven days a week to help address any problem, concern, or emergency that may arise.

Another aspect of customer service is BridgeStreet's relationships with its corporate clients. The company prides itself on meeting business needs and its flexibility in meeting special requests. When one corporation decided to provide its executives with deluxe accommodations complete with luxury linens and larger televisions, BridgeStreet purchased the items on the spot to assure their client's satisfaction.

Consider, for example, the case of Rich Vivirito, controller of downtown Pittsburgh's IKON Document Services and one of BridgeStreet's largest southwestern Pennsylvania customers. "We have trainees coming to town from all over the country. They may stay anywhere from two to four weeks, or even months, and they need accommodations for all that time. BridgeStreet is the most helpful service available," he said. Mr. Vivirito points to BridgeStreet's can-do attitude, where housing specialists work with the client to find the best accommodations, even on a last-minute basis.

"They never say 'No'. Instead, the housing specialists always say, 'Let me see what I can do and get back to you'," Mr. Vivirito said. During his four-year relationship with the accommodation team at BridgeStreet, Mr. Vivirito has come to know them on a first-name basis. That is one of the reasons he prefers dealing with BridgeStreet instead of commercial hotels—even those with closer locations.

Whether working with a major corporation or an individual client, BridgeStreet ensures that its guests are happy—no matter what the location, no matter what the length of stay. It's "a more comfortable way to be away." 𝗣ₐ

Unlike a cramped hotel, a BridgeStreet Accommodations apartment makes guests feel comfortable and at home with spacious living quarters and plenty of room for the family or for entertaining.

BridgeStreet Accommodations, formerly known in Pittsburgh as Temporary Corporate Housing and Corporate Lodgings, provides travelers with "a more comfortable way to be away."

Bayer Corporation

While it's somewhat incongruous for a multinational firm with billions of dollars in sales and tens of thousands of employees in dozens of states to call a single city "home," Pittsburgh is indeed home to Bayer Corporation, the U.S. subsidiary of the worldwide Bayer Group. Bayer is the company that discovered aspirin, polyurethanes and synthetic rubber. Today, it is one of the 100 largest companies in the world.

Bayer was founded more than 130 years ago in a small town in Germany. Shortly thereafter, it established its first American presence with a coal tar dye factory in Albany, New York. It first came to Pittsburgh in the 1950s under the name of Mobay Corporation, a joint venture with the chemical giant Monsanto. Bayer bought out Monsanto in 1967, and its U.S. chemical operations have had their headquarters in Pittsburgh ever since.

Bayer grew in the United States through a series of acquisitions and

Helge H. Wehmeier, President and CEO, Bayer Corporation

mergers, including Miles Laboratories in 1978, which marked Bayer's entry into the U.S. health care arena. In 1992, the company consolidated its U.S. operations under the name of Miles Inc. and made Pittsburgh the corporate headquarters. Three years later, the company reacquired the rights to the Bayer name and the Bayer Cross logo in North America—rights that had been lost after World War I—and Bayer's U.S. operations changed the name to Bayer Corporation. Today the company has businesses in health care and life sciences, chemicals, and imaging technologies.

Pittsburgh has proved a stable home through all of this change, and the people who work at this diversified company take special pride in their home.

Helge H. Wehmeier, a German native, has lived in Pittsburgh since 1991, when he became President and Chief Executive Officer of Bayer Corporation. "Locating our headquarters in Pittsburgh was one of the best decisions we ever made," Mr. Wehmeier says. "Of course, it was not a very difficult decision. Our chemical divisions were very happy to be in Pittsburgh, so we knew it would suit us also."

Bayer's home consists of 16 buildings on a campus in Robinson Township, a suburb of Pittsburgh. The buildings provide some 800,000 square feet of working space for 1,800 Bayer employees. In addition to serving as U.S. corporate headquarters, the campus houses the headquarters of Bayer's four U.S.

chemical divisions: Polymers; Fibers, Additives, and Rubber; Industrial Chemicals; and Performance Products. There are also application development laboratories on the site.

Bayer Corporation's Polymers Division operates a state-of-the-art appliance lab at its Pittsburgh headquarters. This lab is the most comprehensive test facility in North America for testing rigid polyurethane foams used to insulate refrigerator and freezer cabinets. The lab is capable of foaming full-size appliances and is available to Bayer's customers in the appliance industry.

Here Bayer employees develop new technologies and applications for chemical products that give amazing choices to product designers and engineers the world over. In a wide range of product areas—from foams used as refrigerator insulation and in car seats to automotive coatings, the people of Bayer are hard at work developing the next great product. Bayer's products include plastics; pigments; spandex fibers; *Agfa* film; *Advantage* flea control for dogs and cats; the antimicrobial, *Cipro*; the *Glucometer* blood glucose testing products; as well as *Alka-Seltzer* antacid and the flagship *Bayer* Aspirin. Indeed, it is the company's commitment to research and development that accounts for much of its past success and forms the foundation of its future.

One of Pittsburgh's most recognizable landmarks is the Bayer sign on Mt. Washington. Illuminated after dark, the mile of neon tubing brings rotating messages to an estimated quarter million people every day. Messages range from Bayer product promotions to science education quizzes and nonprofit announcements.

But Bayer's community involvement is not limited to a sign. With an overall focus on arts and education, the Bayer Foundation has invested considerable resources in dozens of civic and charitable organizations in the greater Pittsburgh area. Major support has been directed to the Carnegie Science Center and the Pittsburgh Symphony Society, where a novel "Audience of the Future" series seeks to attract young people to the symphony.

The company has also distinguished itself in the promotion of science education—not only in Pittsburgh, but nationwide. Bayer's national Making Science Make Sense Program includes enormously successful hands-on science education programs in Pittsburgh and other Bayer communities and a national public education campaign promoting science literacy. To better implement the program in Pittsburgh, Bayer formed a team called Allegheny Schools Science Education and Technology (ASSET) Inc., which has membership from more than

A Bayer volunteer demonstrates to employees and their children scientific concepts in a fun, hands-on manner.

a dozen Pittsburgh area organizations, including educational institutions, civic groups and other local companies.

Bayer's commitment extends to higher education as well. In 1995, Bayer endowed Duquesne University with a $2 million grant to establish a department which would further the growth of environmental science. The Bayer School of Natural and Environmental Sciences was the company's first academic partnership with a university. "We believe strongly that products need to be manufactured, distributed, used and disposed of in an environmentally responsible manner," says Mr. Wehmeier. "This investment underscores our reliance on science for the development of products, as well as the proper disposal of them."

It's that leadership that carries through to the company's commitment to the United Way. In the last two years, Bayer and its employees have raised well over $1 million for it—$645,000 in 1997 alone. How did they do it? Through a lot of hard work and creative projects like the Haunted Trail, a three- to four-day event on the Bayer campus in which employees do their best to send shivers up and down the spines of community members who pay for the privilege.

Visitors to Bayer's United Way Fall Festival participate in one of many exciting activities, assembling a scarecrow.

But don't get the idea that these employees are not serious about what they do. This company has a fastidious commitment to safety and quality, values that transcend Bayer's operations far beyond Pittsburgh. In addition, the company's *Vision, Values and Beliefs* statement encourages employee participation in all communities where they live and work. They take that commitment seriously. And Pittsburgh is glad they do. 🅿

Washington Plaza

George Washington never slept here. But the father of his country would certainly have envied the lives of those now living in his namesake apartment building--a luxury residential tower with a commanding view above the forks of the Ohio where, as a young soldier, General Washington battled for his nation's independence.

Independence is also a theme that describes the lifestyles of the apartment's more than 600 residents. And every effort is made to assure those residents of the continued freedom to lead their lives with the comfort and style that have made Washington Plaza downtown Pittsburgh's premier residential address since its opening in 1964.

As part of that approach to independent living, building services are operat-

The Washington Plaza residential complex is located in the heart of downtown Pittsburgh, affording residents easy access to work, dining, and entertainment.

ed around the clock to accommodate the distinctive needs of its residents. For example, there is a doorman on duty 24 hours a day. In addition to providing an extra measure of building security, the doorman is available to assist those whose schedules frequently include late-night hours, such as the many interns and physicians who work in the area's nearby hospitals and make their homes in Washington Plaza.

The front desk is also staffed around the clock to offer concierge service whenever a resident needs something outside of normal business hours. The apartment's fully-equipped fitness center, including a sauna and tanning bed, is also available--and in use—24 hours a day. So are the building's self-service laundry room, garage, and TV lounge.

Although just two blocks from one of the most compact and intensively developed central business districts of any major American city, Washington Plaza itself is situated on an attractively

Although located in the heart of Pittsburgh's bustling downtown, the Washington Plaza apartment complex retains the atmosphere of a neighborhood in its own right.

landscaped 4.5-acre property featuring an expansive tree-ringed lawn, shaded picnic tables, barbecue pits, and privacy from surrounding traffic. But the apartment's outdoor space is more than ornamental. It also includes a wide range of athletic and recreational features.

A heated outdoor swimming pool is a central feature of the apartment's suburban-like setting. Two lighted tennis courts are also situated on the property, as is a sand volleyball court. Horseshoe pits are an integral feature of the building's outdoor amenities, and so is a picturesque walking/jogging trail. Active lifestyles are always at home in Washington Plaza.

Several small convenience stores situated inside the building itself help make taking care of life's necessities particularly easy for tenants. A dentist's office, a dry cleaner, a beauty salon, and a deli-market are just a few steps away from any resident's apartment.

What is perhaps most distinctive about Washington Plaza is its location—literally on the edge of downtown Pittsburgh's Golden Triangle. With the corporate headquarters for some of America's leading industrial and financial organizations just a five-minute stroll from their homes, many residents are an easy walk from their offices. The downtown area also offers some of the region's most prestigious retail stores including Saks Fifth Avenue, Brooks Brothers, Lazarus, Kaufmann's, and more.

Restaurants covering the full spectrum of dining styles and tastes are also nearby.

On evenings and weekends, downtown Pittsburgh's Cultural District—home to Heinz Hall, the Benedum, the Byham, the Harris, and soon the O'Reilly

Washington Plaza residents enjoy the amenities of fine living, while keeping the convenience and benefits of a big-city address.

Theatre—comes to life. With its world-class assortment of resident performing arts companies complemented by a steady stream of artists on tour, the Cultural District provides tenants with a non-stop series of attractions — all within minutes of their apartments.

To take full advantage of its location, a Washington Plaza free shuttle van operates to and from key downtown locations every half hour. The van also provides weekly trips to nearby supermarkets for tenants who prefer to leave the driving to others. And for those who don't, indoor and outdoor parking, as well as valet parking for residents and guests, is also available.

Although situated in the heart of one of America's great residential communities, as it evolved over time, Washington Plaza has emerged as a neighborhood in its own right. Its tenants include a healthy balance of long-term residents—including some who moved in when the building first opened—and temporary residents. Singles, couples and young families—those beginning their careers as well as others retired from their professions— provide an eclectic and wholesome mix of neighbors.

The 396 living units range from cozy studio apartments to spacious two-bedroom, two-bath units, as well as a handful of custom-designed, multiple-unit configurations. Several units are leased by nearby corporations, which use them to house employees being transferred into the Pittsburgh area or as temporary housing for other professionals whose assignments in the Pittsburgh area may last several weeks or months in duration.

With the exception of their fully-equipped kitchens, most apartments are rented unfurnished to private individuals. However, furnishings can be provided upon request.

Regardless of their floor plans, all units in the building share certain amenities in common. Unmatched views of the city through floor-to-ceiling windows are one of the building's most striking features. Kitchens featuring frost-free refrigerators, self-cleaning electric ranges, dishwashers, disposals, and full-size microwave ovens are all standard features. Central air conditioning assures

A luxury residential tower, the Washington Plaza offers a commanding view above the forks of the Ohio River.

year-round comfort. And separate storage lockers, as well as 7-day-a-week maintenance service, are also standard.

What is perhaps most surprising is that despite the luxury resort qualities of Washington Plaza living, rentals are remarkably affordable. Studio apartments start from as little as $662 a month, and one-bedroom apartments from $762. Two-bedroom, two-bath units begin at just $1,005. And all rentals include utilities—gas, electricity, water, sewerage and trash collection. Cable television is available; Washington Plaza maintains its own satellite TV reception system with more than 50 channels.

As civic leaders begin implementing their plans for the 21st century, downtown Pittsburgh in the late 1990s stands at the brink of its most ambitious self-renewal program in a generation. In addition to constructing new office towers, stores, athletic facilities, and transportation systems, Pittsburgh is poised to become one of the most attractive central business districts in the nation. It is a rebirth that George Washington himself would have appreciated, and it is one the residents of Washington Plaza are uniquely positioned to enjoy. ℙ

The Westin William Penn: As Grand As Ever

Pittsburgh industrialist Henry Clay Frick set out in 1916 to build the greatest hotel between New York and Chicago.

Today, The Westin William Penn stands resplendent and proud as the grand dame of southwestern Pennsylvania hotels, a national landmark and a favorite of discriminating travelers from around the world.

Completed at a cost of $16 million, the hotel was the last building venture that Frick undertook. In some ways, it is the most steadfast of his Pittsburgh-area undertakings.

It withstood the great St. Patrick's Day flood. It withstood the ascent and the assault of the steel industry, whose airborne effluent was so dense during World War II that women staff members wore satin slips so the dirt wouldn't cling. It stands in fine fashion today,

Built in 1916, today The Westin William Penn is a resplendent national landmark, and a favorite of travelers from around the world.

more than a decade after the steel industry that Frick helped build receded from the region's riverbanks to relocate in more favorable labor climates closer to prime markets.

Under the city's cleared skies and beside its three cleansed rivers where pleasure boats and sport fishermen have replaced blast furnaces and foundrymen, The Westin William Penn stands in its Italianate architectural grandeur, wrapped in creamy terra cotta topped by red brick, still drawing travelers through its awe-inspiring Palm Court Lobby. There actress Lillian Russell, William Penn, descendant of Pennsylvania's founder, and Frick himself helped celebrate opening night.

It was quintessential Pittsburgh circa 1916: The steel in the hotel's framing as well as the piping, cement, brick and bathtubs came from the ground, mills and factories around Pittsburgh. Yet the opulence of its furnishings and the fussing of the staff spoke of the vast fortunes extracted from the muscle and mineral wealth of the region.

The hotel became the venue of power politics, popular entertainment and pure ostentation.

In 1917, former President Teddy Roosevelt told a throng of listeners in the lobby to "buck up for America."

President Harry Truman used to slip out the side door for a solitary evening walk. Richard Nixon summoned a bellman to bring a bottle of scotch to his room, then invited the bellman to join him for a drink.

The hotel was the second home of David L. Lawrence, popular Pittsburgh mayor, Pennsylvania governor, Democratic kingmaker and impetus for the renaissance that scraped the city skyline and riverbanks clean of industrial grit in the 1950s. Financier Richard K. Mellon was on a first-name basis with the bellmen.

The hotel's Terrace Room featured the torch singer Hildegarde, who insisted on bathing in buttermilk.

Newcomer Lawrence Welk played the hotel's Italian Terrace on New Year's Eve 1938 and accepted a Pittsburgh woman's contest entry—"Bubbles in the Wine"—as the name of his theme song. A year later, Welk came back and adopted the bubble background created by house engineer Ludwig Dernoshek using a fan, an old clock motor, a sardine can, a pie pan, and liquid soap.

The Westin William Penn is ideal for business travelers, featuring spacious guest rooms with plenty of space for working as well as resting.

On his visit, Jackie Gleason arrived at the door in an open convertible, surrounded by the June Taylor dancers.

The Continental Bar sold more than 500 Old Fashioneds a day, and the Urban Room orchestra played dance music until 6 o'clock each morning.

Through the ebb and flow of business tides, The Westin William Penn has emerged on the threshold of a new century with the staff and technology to meet the service- and quality-minded expectations of this age amid the grandeur of an earlier one. ▣

Community College of Allegheny County

S ince opening its doors in the fall of 1966, the Community College of Allegheny County has enriched the lives of more than two million people—a number roughly equivalent to Allegheny County's entire population.

The largest school of its type in Pennsylvania and one of the most fully developed community colleges in the nation, CCAC's record is marked by dramatic growth in every area of operation: enrollment, facilities, academic offerings, career development, and service to students.

Founded by the Allegheny County Board of Commissioners to help Pittsburgh-area residents upgrade their skills and improve their lives, CCAC offers specifically career-oriented programs in more than 100 applied disciplines. Two-year programs leading to degrees or certificates are offered for studies in business, health, social services, applied arts, service technologies, and engineering.

ferable to most western Pennsylvania colleges as well as to a number of others outside the state. In fact, many students enroll with the intention of entering a four-year school as a junior after earning an Associate Degree at CCAC.

During the 1996-97 academic year, more than 25,000 of CCAC's 85,000+ students were enrolled for credit in academic programs. More than two-thirds were enrolled in community service and continuing education courses. Self-help, personal enrichment, and life skills classes remain major attractions. As a result, CCAC's student profile is unlike that of most traditional colleges. The median age is 28; 60 percent are women, and 40 percent are evening students. Nearly 15 percent come from minority populations.

The Community College of Allegheny County's main campus offers career-oriented programs in more than 100 applied disciplines, two-year degree and certificate programs, and a variety of continuing education classes.

CCAC is equipped with up-to-date computing systems. All students have access to the World Wide Web and an e-Mail address. This technology is complemented with classes offered over the Internet and distance learning systems that enable students to pursue their studies at home.

Community College of Allegheny County becomes a part of the lives of thousands each year. In an average year, about one in every ten Allegheny County residents is enrolled at CCAC. As one of the premier community colleges in Pennsylvania, CCAC is committed to preparing its students for success in a highly competitive and rapidly changing world. **P̲a̲**

CCAC students can complete two-year programs leading to degrees or certificates in a wide range of studies including business, health, social services, applied arts, service technologies, and engineering.

At the same time, CCAC provides a full range of academic programs that parallel those offered in the first two years at a traditional liberal arts college. Credits from these CCAC courses are fully trans-

Whatever their profile, CCAC students find its programs to be among the region's most affordable. Tuition for Allegheny County residents is only $68 per credit. Many students are eligible for financial aid, which totals approximately $10 million a year.

With four major campuses and eight off-campus centers, CCAC classes are easily accessible to students throughout Allegheny County. Altogether, the college maintains more than a million square feet of classroom space on its 350 acres. Other instructional facilities include laboratories, art and music studios, theaters, libraries, athletic facilities, and student centers.

Greene County

I f that old adage of the real estate business still holds true that the three most important considerations for determining the value and salability of property are location, location, and location then Greene County is, to borrow the nickname of neighboring West Virginia, "Almost Heaven."

Local boosters say Greene County is truly blessed in the location department, situated as it is on a major interstate highway between Pittsburgh to the north and Morgantown, West Virginia, to the south. What's more, they point out, Greene, covering an area of 578 square miles, has the smallest county population in the region and has plenty of well-situated land sitting vacant and available for development, especially along the interstate.

Interstate 79's interchanges in the county are mostly undeveloped. And because development along the interstate in Allegheny and Butler counties to the north and in West Virginia south to Morgantown has proceeded at a steady pace in recent years, Greene's are among a very few remaining undeveloped interchange parcels on the highway. That means there is a tremendous potential for economic development there.

County leaders are eager to tap that potential. They see it as a means of diversifying Greene's economic base, which for most of this century has been anchored to coal. (The county's first deep mine, the H.P. Dilworth Mine near Rices Landing, opened in 1902.) How deeply embedded is that anchor? Coal is Greene's dominant industry and coal mining is its biggest employment category. Coal companies' taxes today cover about half the county's budget and the budgets of several Greene school districts as well. Greene County's coal lands are the richest in the state and are among the richest in the country. Greene still has four billion tons of bituminous coal reserves and is tapping them at the rate of about thirty-three million tons a year. The Bailey/Enlow Fork Mine in north-

Greene County has a wealth of opportunity in its land and economic resources, making it a great place to live, work, and raise a family. Photo by Kevin Cooke/Graule Studios

western Greene (practically straddling the Washington-Greene border) is the largest underground mine in the world in terms of production.

On the surface, Greene does not appear to be an economic base in critical need of diversification. But it is, for a couple of reasons.

One is the tax situation. Coal companies pay a lot of taxes but the taxes are based on the amount of coal reserves they own, not on how much coal they produce. So as coal is mined, the tax base shrinks, even as new production records are being set thanks to advances in mining technology.

And that is another reason for actively seeking industrial diversification. Technology, particularly in the form of longwall equipment, is displacing humans in mining. Using sophisticated equipment, companies can mine more coal with fewer people. That has resulted in a steady decline in the number of mining jobs in the county, even as new production records are being set. There are thirty-one thousand fewer bituminous coal mining jobs than there were fifteen years ago.

(In 1995, mines in Greene and Washington counties produced more than half the coal mined in Pennsylvania. There are forty-six underground bituminous mines in Pennsylvania and nine of them employ longwall technology. All nine are in Greene and Washington counties.)

Although coal has long dominated Greene's economy, it was a relative latecomer to the county's industrial scene. There was evidence that there was coal in the area before the Revolutionary War, but it attracted little attention. The area's forests provided an abundant supply of wood for fuel and only a few coal-containing parcels along the Monongahela River had been sold before about 1895.

Long before that, in the 1780s, whiskey

distilling was an important business for the area's farmers, who found it cheaper and more convenient to ship the liquor they distilled from their grain than the bulky grain itself. (A pack horse could handle a load of only about five or six bushels of grain but could easily carry the liquor distilled from twenty-four bushels.) There were seventy licensed distilleries in the area by 1783. Whiskey making became an important business for the area's farmers—so important that they rebelled when the federal government imposed a tax on liquor in 1791.

Coal is Greene County's dominant industry and coal mining is its biggest employment category. Photo by Kevin Cooke/Graule Studios

In 1790, six years before the establishment of Greene as a county, glass making was introduced to the area when immigrant German glassblowers set up shop in Greensboro to make window glass. The discovery of deposits of special types of clay near Carmichaels soon led to the making of glassware and fine pottery.

Oil and natural gas were important resources before coal was mined in the area. The first oil well near Carmichaels was brought in in 1822 and the first natural gas well was drilled near Mt. Morris in 1878.

Early industrial growth in the county was slow because of the lack of adequate transportation routes. Communities along the river on the eastern border (the Monongahela River serves as Greene's eastern border with Fayette County) prospered but those in the interior lagged behind because they had no major roads, railroads, or rivers to rely on.

Today the county is much better and more thoroughly served by highways and railways. Besides Interstate 79, which is central Greene's principal north-south transportation link, the county relies on U.S. Route 19 and busy state routes 18, 21, 88, 188, and 221.

Big, lumbering coal trucks are familiar sights along those roadways and their loads reflect coal's continued importance to Greene's economy. Mine employment

The landscape of Greene County is dotted with a number of historic covered bridges. Photo courtesy the Greene County Tourist Promotion Agency

may be declining at a rapid rate, but more than 23 percent of the county's work force still work in mines, according to state Department of Labor and Industry records. Those records also show that the county's other current major employment categories are service, retailing, agriculture (Greene is the state's largest sheep-growing county), and state government. The county's state government payroll is substantial mostly because Greene is home to two state prisons: the six-year-old State Correctional Institution Greene, which employs more than six hundred people, and a minimum-security lockup in Waynesburg, the county seat, which employs three hundred to four hundred.

SCI Greene has had a major economic impact on the county. Building the facility provided a number of very well paying construction jobs and the construction project included about $20 million in infrastructure improvements, particularly a water plant upgrade and expansion of a sewage treatment facility in Franklin Township. Those improvements, although required by the prison, are now assets very beneficial to the county's further economic development efforts. And staffing the prison, requiring the hiring of hundreds of people, was one of the reasons why Greene has enjoyed a population growth of more than 6 percent since the start of the decade—the second

largest such increase in the region after Butler County.

Another major contributor to Greene's population growth has been Waynesburg College, which has expanded course offerings and increased faculty and staff positions appreciably.

Jobs and job opportunities were what brought the new people to the county; the county's amenities are what are keeping them there and keeping them pleased with their new homes. Greene offers a relatively laid-back, rural lifestyle, reasonable land and housing prices, and good schools. Ryerson Station State Park in Richill Township, state game lands, and several public and private parks and recreational facilities offer residents abundant opportunities for outdoor activities.

Parks of a different sort— business/industrial parks—are adding increased job opportunities to that list of amenities. Since the diversification effort began in earnest several years ago, county officials, aided by agencies like Greene's Industrial Development Authority and Industrial Development Corporation, have attracted a number of new jobs to the county and have had a big hand in retaining companies already resident there.

About four hundred new jobs have come to Greene in the past five years. About half that number are at at a Japanese-owned plastics injection molding plant that opened in 1992 to make consoles for a television plant in Westmoreland County. (Development officials point out that, besides being a job generator, the console plant serves as a fine example of regional economic development, with Greene benefitting from a major, long-established development in Westmoreland.) Located in Waynesburg at the I-79 interchange, the plastics plant is an example of the type of development officials hope to generate on now vacant parcels along the interstate.

Waynesburg College has been a major contributor to Greene County's population, drawing students with expanded course offerings as well as increased faculty and staff positions. Photo by Kevin Cooke/Graule Studios

That is why county leaders are excited about the Meadow Ridge Industrial Park being built at the I-79 Mt. Morris interchange just this side of Greene's border with West Virginia. A West Virginia company looking for growing room has signed on as anchor tenant of the 130-acre park, which is jointly owned by the Regional Industrial Development Corporation and the Greene County Industrial Development Authority.

Two new companies are moving in to the Paisley Industrial Park in Carmichaels, owned by the Greene Industrial Development Corporation. There also is a publicly owned industrial park at the Waynesburg I-79 interchange. There presently are no privately owned business parks in the county.

Building industrial parks and providing quality land for development are key economic development strategies but

Agriculture is still one of Greene County's major employment categories, with Greene being the state's largest sheep-growing county. Photo by Kevin Cooke/Graule Studios

they are not the only strategies Greene officials are employing in their efforts to diversify and revitalize the county's economy. The county also has embarked on a job training/adult retraining program with two goals: provide realistic technology training to high school students and retrain downsized workers, not only ex-miners but others as well whose job skills, though considerable, are not necessarily transferable to the new types of employment opportunities becoming available. A consortium of Waynesburg College, county govern-

ment, and local education leaders called the Greene County Education Foundation is in charge of the county-wide program, which many feel is unique in the region for its breadth and its scope.

Whether it is land or buildings or financial incentives or hard-working, skilled, and loyal workers, Greene County is determined to provide what it takes to attract new companies and new jobs into the area and give its established employers the help they need to grow, expand, and stay competitive. **Pa**

Chapter

8

Indiana County

Y ou could say that seeing the sights in Indiana County has its ups and downs. "Up" is the highest (1,216 feet) smokestack in the United States at the Homer City Electric Generating Station in the south central section of the county. "Down" is Conemaugh Gap in the county's southeastern corner, the deepest (1,350 feet) gorge east of the Mississippi River.

Both the gorge and the smokestack are important to Indiana County's economic vitality. The seven-mile-long Conemaugh Gap, cut by the Conemaugh River through Laurel Ridge Mountain, is one of the stellar attractions of the county's tourism business. And the Homer City smokestack is a towering symbol of the county's electric power generating capabilities that help bestow legitimacy on Indiana's claim of being the "Energy Heartland of Pennsylvania."

Indiana County is a major supplier of electric energy and the county's three power generating stations—Keystone, Homer City, and Conemaugh—together

In contrast to its busy economic picture, Indiana County is predominantly rural, ranking third largest in area of the region's ten counties, but third smallest in population. Photo by Kevin Cooke/Graule Studios

burn on average almost two thousand tons of coal every hour to produce the electricity shipped to utility customers not only in Pennsylvania but also in New York, New Jersey, Maryland, Delaware, and Washington, D.C.

One of the stations, Keystone, is even a tourist attraction. Visitors to the Keystone Overlook, a staffed observation area overlooking the station, can picnic while they take in the panoramic view of the station and the surrounding area and learn about coal-fired electric generation.

The stations used to get most of their coal from local mines and coal mining was one of the county's earliest and most dynamic industries. But coal has slipped considerably in recent years. Since 1985, the county has lost about four thousand mining and related jobs. Yet, a not insignificant percentage of Indiana County's workforce, almost 7 percent,

still is engaged in mining—the second highest concentration of coal mining jobs in the region after Greene County. And there are still more than 400 million tons of good quality bituminous coal sleeping silently beneath the county's rolling hills, waiting for a resurgence in demand for what once was called "black gold."

Before coal came to prominence in Indiana County, there was salt. Salt mining and refining were the first industries in the Kiskiminetas River valley, which starts in the southwestern corner of the county and extends into Armstrong County. Salt was discovered in 1812 near what was to become, appropriately enough, the town of Saltsburg and the first salt wells were drilled there a year later. Many salt wells were located along the Conemaugh and Kiskiminetas rivers.

Indiana County's electric power generating capabilities have earned the county yet another nickname, "Energy Heartland of Pennsylvania." Photo by Kevin Cooke/Graule Studios

Other important early industries included iron smelting, grain grinding, alcohol distilling, hide tanning, boat building, and lumbering. The area's first gristmill was built in 1773 and there were four stone blast furnaces built in the area. The Eliza Furnace, which operated in the 1840s near the county's southeastern border with Cambria County producing pig iron for the Pittsburgh market, has been preserved as a tourist attraction.

Early industries thrived because it was inexpensive to transport coal, salt, and manufactured products to market. Initially, the county's rivers did the job and they were soon augmented by turnpikes and toll roads. Later came the canal: the Pennsylvania Main Line Canal linking Pittsburgh and Philadelphia cut through southwestern Indiana County. Later still came the railroads.

Towns thrived because of their location. Blairsville had the good fortune to be situated at the junction of the Conemaugh River and the Northern Pike, and so became an important manufacturing, mining, and transportation center. Its prominence as a transportation hub was enhanced in 1851, when the Pennsylvania Railroad opened a branch line, and further in 1860, when the Western Pennsylvania Railroad was organized there.

Examples of the county's transportation, industrial, and mining heritage are being preserved. The Tunnelview Historic Site between Saltsburg and Blairsville houses remnants of the Pennsylvania Canal and railroad facilities. Canal Park in Saltsburg, which was an important stop on the canal, contains artifacts and exhibits related to the canal and also to salt drilling, glass making, and boat building. Two old mining company towns have been preserved: the village of Commodore, founded in 1919 as

Indiana County is a major supplier of electric energy through three power generating stations - Keystone, Homer City, and Conemaugh. Photo by Kevin Cooke/Graule Studios

one of few towns in the early 1900s with sewage and running water, and Iselin, built in 1903, where miners' homes, the mine office, a doctor's office, and the infamous company store are preserved.

As coal and salt have declined, another natural resource has moved to the economic forefront: trees—specifically evergreens, and even more specifically Christmas trees. The growing, harvesting, and marketing of Chrinstmas trees—millions of them every year—is one of the county's main businesses and has led to the adoption of yet another county motto: "Christmas Tree Capital of the World."

Indiana County's climate, topography, soil, and moisture are ideally suited for growing various species of evergreens—much better suited, in fact, than they are for large-scale, conventional crop farming. That took its toll on many family farms and freed up large tracts of cleared land that could be converted to evergreen growing. The cultivation of Christmas trees as a farm crop in the county started around 1918 and became a major economic asset starting in the 1930s.

Commercial evergreen growing requires space and Indiana County has space to spare. Predominantly rural, Indiana is the third largest in size (825 square miles) of the region's ten counties but ranks third smallest in population, with only about 109 people per square mile (compared to 265 people per square mile statewide). Most of its residents live in the southwest part along the U.S. Route 119 corridor and along state Route 286, the two principal north-south roads that link the sector with the county seat, Indiana Borough.

That area is expected to absorb most of an anticipated population growth over the next three decades. According to projections, Indiana's population, now slightly more than 90,000, should grow by about 4,500 people by the year 2000 and reach almost 103,000 by the year 2020.

Men and women in the 20-to-44 age group comprise the largest population block in the county (39 percent) and the biggest segment of its labor force. Currently, the biggest percentage of that force works in retailing (23 percent), service industries (20 percent, with 44 percent of those in health care), and manufacturing (almost 12 percent). And each of these categories has grown recently, however modestly.

Construction was the category showing the biggest one-year growth (22 percent-

Indiana County has many educational opportunities, and is home to Indiana University of Pennsylvania, the largest of Pennsylvania's state-owned universities. Photo by Kevin Cooke/Graule Studios

plus) in the latest state Department of Labor and Industry employment report. Many of those new jobs were on a project to build a new state juvenile detention facility in White Township. When completed in 1999, the facility also will have a longer-term impact on employment in the county: it is expected to employ 250 people with starting salaries averaging $25,000. It is estimated that the facility will pump at least $10 million annually

into the local economy.

The employment-growth trend is expected to continue and even accelerate because Indiana County has a lot to offer businesses, including a population with an attractive youth-age balance; a resilient, eager, increasingly skilled, and increasingly better-educated labor pool (the percentage of high school and college graduates is growing steadily); low utility rates, housing costs, and living costs; a quiet, unhurried rural environment; reasonable proximity to Pittsburgh; and good educational opportunities.

Indiana University of Pennsylvania, with its main campus in the county seat, is the largest of Pennsylvania's state-

owned universities and its internship program is the largest in the state. IUP's graduate schools and vocational-technical programs help students acquire job skills and provide businesses with trained workers. So do area vocational and technical schools, which work closely with private businesses and the county's secondary education system.

Indiana also is developing a vibrant business and industrial park system. Currently there are seven industrial parks in the county—one county-owned (Commerce Park); one owned by the Center for Economic Operations, the county's economic development agency (Corporate Campus); and five privately owned and operated.

Commerce Park, located near the new IUP south campus, is attracting interest from outside firms thinking of relocating in the county as well as from resident businesses looking for room to expand operations. At the 100-acre Corporate

Indiana County is the home town of late movie legend Jimmy Stewart. The airport is named for him, and there is a statue of him and a Jimmy Stewart Museum in downtown Indiana near where the actor's father operated a hardware store. Photo courtesy the Center for Economic Operations of Indiana County

Campus in Burrell Township not far from Blairsville, infrastructure work is being completed and a 30,000-square-foot business incubator/innovation center is being built there. Between 150 and 200 new jobs are projected for the center over the next few years.

Highways long ago replaced the rivers as the county's main access routes to the rich markets that surround it and it is rather well served by its roadway system. It has more state-owned roads than any other county in Pennsylvania. U.S. Route 119 bisects the county north-to-south and U.S. 422 divides the county on

an east-west line. U.S. 22 and State Route 286 serve the southern portion of county. The county sits roughly midway between Interstate 80 in the north and Interstate 76, the Pennsylvania Turnpike, to the south, and is linked via Route 422 with Interstate 79, fifty miles to the west. Significant and extensive improvements are needed in the county's highway system if Indiana hopes to achieve its development and job-growth goals, and government, business, and economic development leaders are lobbying hard to get major road construction projects under way. And because so many businesses now rely as heavily on air transportation as they do on highways in their operations, officials also are seeking funds to make major improvements to the county's airport, named for native son movie actor Jimmy Stewart. (There also is a Jimmy Stewart Museum in downtown Indiana near where the actor's father operated a hardware store).

Indiana County is beginning to attract attention as well as new businesses and new jobs. It won recognition as the 1997 Outstanding Pennsylvania Community by the Pennsylvania Chamber of Business and Industry for, among other things, its economic development initiatives, its success in attracting the new juvenile detention facility, the Corporate Campus/innovation center development, and the success of the county's public-private partnerships. ◪

Modern modes of transportation long ago replaced rivers as the county's access routes to surrounding markets.
Photo by Kevin Cooke/Graule Studios

Indiana University of Pennsylvania

Why is it that applications for admission to Indiana University of Pennsylvania—a venerable, state-owned university forty miles northeast of Pittsburgh—have been soaring since the mid-1990s? The answer, as university President Lawrence K. Pettit explains, involves a number of factors.

Certainly part of it has to do with a growing public recognition of IUP as a leading institution in Pennsylvania and, increasingly, on the national stage as well. For example, a number of stories now carried by the major national media are based on research conducted at IUP. Leading news publications are also seeking out IUP faculty members for their comments and insights on a wide range of current issues.

At the same time, commercially published college guidebooks have begun to note with interest the university's many strengths. Other widely circulated publications, including *Barrons,*

| **IUP students receive a mixture of Liberal Studies and specialized instruction that prepares them for life as educated adults.**

Money Magazine, and *U.S. News and World Report*, have starting placing IUP among their nationally ranked institutions, where it compares very favorably.

Another reason for IUP's rapid rise from a regional institution to national prominence is reflected in its physical plant. A major capital campaign, concluded at the end of 1998, enabled IUP to fund an ambitious series of restorations and improvements. Today, all of the university's academic and residential buildings are connected by a high-capacity fiber optic cable system. In addition to streamlining registration and improving security, the system gives students immediate access to scholarship, to entertainment, and to one another, whether across the hall or across the country.

A new building housing the Eberly College of Business—the university's first new structure in more than a decade—was completed in 1996. Major renovations to several other facilities have helped to extend their capabilities and renew their vitality as fixtures of campus life. And, in what President Pettit calls the most important IUP development in thirty years, the 1995 purchase of a 137-acre tract adjacent to campus will allow the university to expand during the coming decades as its needs and resources allow.

Certainly one of the major reasons for IUP's prominence stems from its long-established emphasis on excellence in teaching. Unlike many state-owned universities, IUP does not use graduate students to teach its undergraduate classes. At the same time, the great majority of those classes are small. More than a

| **Students have thrived under Indiana University of Pennsylvania's tutelage since 1875, when the school was established as Indiana Normal School.**

quarter of all undergraduate classes have ten or fewer students, allowing for a high level of interaction and individual attention.

What is taught in these classrooms is also fundamental to IUP's students appeal. Throughout its curriculum, the university places a strong emphasis on the liberal arts. No matter which undergraduate majors its students might elect, Liberal Studies courses will help to familiarize them with the body of knowledge, critical thinking, and lifelong learning skills that are requisite to being an educated adult.

Simultaneously, however, all IUP programs in every academic unit are focused on preparing students for real careers in the real world. That focus is sharpest in the university's specialized schools. For instance, at the Eberly College of Business, faculty members with backgrounds in business, scholarship, and teaching offer programs that include accounting, finance, management, marketing, and information systems. In the College of Education, students become certified for professional work in numerous teaching specialties and in allied areas of research. Likewise, the university's academic colleges—Fine Arts, Health and Human Services, Humanities and Social Sciences, and Natural Sciences and Mathematics—each provide their students with the foundations for professional careers as well as for further study at the graduate level.

The university's innovative Robert E. Cook Honors College, which opened in 1994 through the generosity of a graduate for whom the school is named, builds on IUP's established strengths in teaching. Featuring a newly remodeled facility where as many as 200 students can live and study, the College offers an environment where its most talented students can maintain a particularly close collaborative relationship with one another and with some of the university's most respected faculty members. Independence, self-direction, exploration, and intellectual growth are the hallmarks of this special program, which is open to students in every major.

Beyond the university's distinguishing scholarly and physical assets, there is another reason for the sharp growth in IUP's application rate—one that is intensely practical. It is that the cost of attending IUP is significantly lower than at virtually any of the state's privately owned colleges. Providing the state's greatest value in higher education at the lowest possible cost is part of a deliberate strategy to build on the university's growing national reputation. But to make sure money does not become a barrier to entry, fully 80 percent of the undergradu-

ates attending IUP also receive some form of financial aid.

In 1875, when IUP first opened as Indiana Normal School with 368 students, its assignment was to prepare suitably qualified teachers for careers in the commonwealth's public schools. Over time, as its facilities expanded and student body grew, so did the school's mission. During the mid-1960s, in recognition of its evolving role, the school—which had by then become Indiana State College—changed its name once again, this time to Indiana University of Pennsylvania.

Today, IUP's original 1875 building still stands at the heart of its traditional, tree-lined campus. But its enrollment of

Academic excellence is attracting attention to IUP as a leading institution in Pennsylvania as well as the nation.

IUP enrolls some 13,500 students, including undergraduates in more than a hundred majors, as well as graduate students at both the master's degree and doctoral degree levels.

13,500 now includes undergraduates in more than a hundred different majors as well as graduate students enrolled in forty separate master's degree and eight different doctoral degree programs.

About four thousand IUP students live on campus. Fourteen secure dormitories and two apartment buildings provide a wide range of living options. Intensified study floors, smoke-free residence halls, and academic specialty floors are among the residential choices. Four separate dining facilities provide a wide range of food selections. And a variety of other resources are available for extra curricular recreational, artistic, or scholarly pursuits.

This distinctive combination of physical and intellectual resources has triggered a surge in applications for admission to IUP and, at the threshold of the new millennium, thrust it into the ranks of America's nationally rated universities. **P**

Indiana Hospital

Being the only acute-care facility in Indiana County is a major responsibility—one that Indiana Hospital takes very seriously. Throughout the years, however, the specific expectations have changed. As a result, the hospital has periodically reassessed its own operations, making sure they remain focused on meeting the evolving health care needs of Indiana County residents.

During 1997, the hospital went through its most recent, and most extensive, strategic planning initiative since its doors first opened in 1914. Through that process, a new vision for the hospital emerged. It is based on the shared recognition that a combination of changes in health care delivery, technology, finance, and philosophy have created a new world of opportunity for health care pro-

As the only acute-care facility in Indiana County, Indiana Hospital meets a wide variety of needs through many avenues of service ranging from providing emergency and surgical patient care to conducting wellness and educational programs.

fessionals and consumers. Today, in a marketplace characterized by a growing number of health, fitness, and lifestyle choices, Indiana Hospital is determined to remain the preferred health services provider for residents in its service area.

By offering a wide range of services at the hospital and its network of satellite locations, Indiana Hospital is able to make top-quality medical care available for all of the county's residents at every stage of their lives. With 130 acute-care beds and 155 physicians on staff, the hospital offers general medical care, obstetric and pediatric care, geriatric mental health and surgical services, intensive and emergency care, and, through its Transitional Care Center, short-term skilled nursing care for patients who are not yet able to return home or to another facility.

Other services offered by Indiana Hospital include such specialized programs as cardiac rehabilitation, occupational health, and treatment of sleep disorders. A Geriatric Care Center, with 14 beds, provides short-term comprehensive

care to patients 55 years or older who have psychiatric and physical health problems related to aging.

The hospital also owns and operates several off-site primary-care practices. Offering a wide range of healthcare services and extended office hours, these practices are designed to provide access to care in the county's outlying areas. Other preventive and educational programs offered by the hospital deal with babysitting, prenatal guidance, arthritis, and diabetes.

Working with various community agencies and other health care organizations is another way the hospital ensures access to services for all area residents.

As part of its outreach strategy, Indiana Hospital is affiliated with both the Visiting Nurse Association of Indiana County—an independent agency providing comprehensive home health services—and The Open Door, a counseling center addressing drug and alcohol abuse, as well as other mental health issues. Also serving outpatients is a 48,000-square-foot ambulatory surgery center/physician office building on the hospital grounds.

These affiliations and alliances, together with the hospital's prestigious "Accreditation with Commendation" from the Joint Commission on Accreditation of Healthcare Organizations, reflect Indiana Hospital's ongoing commitment to comprehensive, high-quality health care services. And they confirm the hospital's continuing role as the county's primary source for health care.

FMC Corporation

F MC Corporation's Material Handling Equipment Operation, located in Homer City, Pennsylvania, has manufactured high-performance bulk material handling and parts handling equipment for more than sixty years. Material Handling equipment is used by many different industries to feed, convey, elevate, orient, and position products as they are processed into consumable goods.

When Herr Foods wanted to convey its potato chips from the oven to the packaging line without damage, they relied on FMC's Food Handling expertise to design and build the appropriate conveyor solution. When Consolidated Coal needed to move thousands of tons of coal per hour from anthracite mines to waiting railcars, Syntron Feeders were manufactured to deliver the load. And when Eastman Kodak's film-making operation required parts-feeding equipment to feed and orient film spools, end caps, and film canisters to high-speed assembly operations, they turned to FMC's skilled bowl toolers to produce the automated solution.

Divided into four distinct business groups, each unit of FMC's Material Handling Equipment Operation is keenly focused on the specific needs of its customers. The Food Handling Equipment Business Unit, for example, provides conveying, screening, grading, and elevating solutions for food processors such as Frito Lay, Kelloggs, and Quaker Oats.

In the industrial products environment, the Heavy Products Business Unit produces industrial feeders and screens used in mines, rock quarries, steel mills, glass plants, and numerous other harsh environments. The General Products Business Unit provides flow valves, bin vibrators, and light capacity feeders for a wide range of applications including pharmaceutical, food, and chemical handling applications. And the Parts Handling Business Unit manufactures

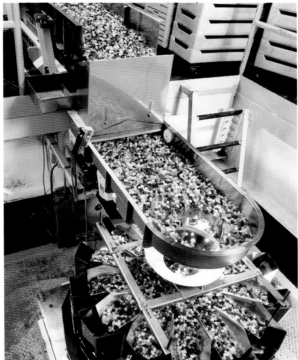

FMC Syntron food conveyor and feeder distributing candy to packaging scales.

vibrating, rotary, and linear parts feeders for diverse industries including automotive, fasteners, pharmaceuticals, consumer products, and electronics.

FMC's current workforce is approximately 400 in its 275,000-square-foot manufacturing facility in Indiana County. Manufacturing processes include functions such as machining, forming, finishing, and assembly. A dedicated R&D staff, as well as complete engineering and design services, support current and future product offerings.

FMC's Material Handling Equipment Operation originated in 1921 in Pittsburgh, Pennsylvania, as the National Electric Manufacturing Company. The name was changed to Syntron when it moved to its present location in Homer City in 1937. Syntron was acquired by Link-Belt in the mid-1950s, then became a part of FMC

Corporation in 1967. In addition to the Homer City plant, the Material Handling Equipment Operation maintains manufacturing facilities in Anaheim, California, and Fakenham, England.

Today, FMC Corporation's Material Handling Equipment Operation holds the National Safety Council's "Best Record Award" for Safety in its Standard Industrial Code category. In addition to its exemplary safety record, 65 percent of FMC's employees maintain an outstanding attendance record by missing less than eight hours of work per year. The operation is also ISO 9001 certified, indicative of FMC's ongoing commitment to produce products of high quality and performance.

Although FMC's customer base has historically been North American, there is a growing market for bulk material handling equipment in Latin America and other parts of the world. FMC maintains a dedicated sales force in the United States and Europe, as well as a worldwide network of licensees and representatives to promote and sell FMC Material Handling Equipment in the global marketplace. **Pa**

FMC Syntron heavy-duty feeder moving rock to a crushing operation.

Indiana County Chamber of Commerce

Traditionally known as the Christmas Tree Capital of the world. Boyhood home of actor Jimmy Stewart. Scenic covered bridges. Picturesque rolling hills. These are among the charms for which Indiana County is known by local residents. But informing the outside world of these attractions is the job of the Indiana County Chamber of Commerce—an association of local leaders for whom the county's scenic assets also represent potential business assets. And their message is getting out.

But while promoting the county's scenic business assets is an important part of the Chamber's mission, it is only one aspect of the Chamber's work. Another involves initiatives that strengthen Indiana County's industrial and infrastructure base. For example, in conjunction with the Indiana County Board of Commissioners, Indiana County Development Corporation, Indiana University of Pennsylvania, and the Indiana County Tourist Bureau, the Chamber is a part of Indiana County's Center for Economic Operations, referred to as the CEO. This partnership of leading county organizations has enabled the

Indiana County's scenic amenities are also an asset to drawing business and new residents.

county to develop a business assistance delivery system which serves to strengthen those companies already here and new companies and businesses looking to locate in the county.

Surprisingly, especially in light of its current business development and membership services focus, the Chamber didn't always make strengthening the local economy its highest priority. In fact, when it was founded in 1912 by a group of prominent Indiana County businessmen, the Chamber served as a purely social club and continued operate that way for some years.

But its mission became serious when, in the 1940s, the county suffered an economic crisis. Coal mining—long the mainstay of Indiana County's economy—had stumbled. Unemployment due to the drop in coal production became an overwhelming concern of the area. In response, several dedicated businessmen began working through the Chamber to help rebuild the economy. They began by establishing the Indiana Community Development Corporation and a sister organization, the Greater Indiana Development Corporation. Along with the Chamber, these organizations became vehicles to raise capital for industrial development. Through their efforts, Indiana County was not only able to attract new industry to the area, it was also able to help existing companies grow and expand.

Then, during the early 1960s, the Chamber established a financial division to assist businesses and industries relocating to Indiana County. To date more than $4 million has been raised by the Chamber to further economic development in the county. Its board of directors was expanded to include representation from communities county wide. Volunteer committees sup-

Residents of Indiana County value their history as a strong foundation for a bright future.

plemented the Chamber's industrial development efforts with their own community and educational projects.

Today, more than 720 businesses and community members belong to the Chamber. According to its president, Dana P. Henry, the Chamber remains focused on developing and promoting the economic, business, and public interests of Indiana County. Its stated goals include: assisting existing businesses and industry; assisting with economic growth; providing information about the county to interested businesses and residents; and promoting community pride throughout the region. Chamber Chairman Domenic P. Rocco, Jr., Brigadier General, U.S. Army (Ret.) proudly expresses its mission statement as: "Fighting for Economic Growth! Fighting for Jobs!"

Chairman Rocco, Jr., has observed that just as Indiana County values the legacy represented by its past, the county will be an integral part of the nation's economic future. As a result, the Indiana County Chamber of Commerce will continue to be a major contributor toward this effort. **Pa**

Clark Metal Products

Chances are, when you look at any of the most widely-used process control equipment, high-end laboratory instruments, electric service panels, or medical electronic devices, the first thing you see is its metal enclosure. And for dozens of sophisticated equipment makers throughout the mid-Atlantic region, those enclosures come from Clark Metal Products—a specialty maker of custom metal parts located in Blairsville, Indiana County.

Crafting the cabinets, racks and other metal components for precision instruments and advanced electronics is itself an exacting assignment. Tolerances can be extremely tight. So can turnaround times. Quality expectations are exceptionally high. And the ability to withstand extreme operating conditions while protecting sensitive interior parts is fundamental.

Good design is basic to meeting those demands, and it comes about in several ways. For most of the parts Clark produces, a complete set of drawings and design specifications has already been prepared by the customer before actual

Leading the Clark Metal Products team are, from left, Jack Clark, President; Dave Clark, Jr., Sales Manager; Dave Clark, Sr., Vice President; and Rob Clark, Operations Manager.

construction begins. In some cases, the customer provides rough sketches, which Clark engineers refine prior to production. In a few instances, customers will ask Clark to design and fabricate an enclosure to house their product. Whatever the request, experienced Clark professionals are equipped to use the company's in-house AUTOCAD capabilities to prepare final drawings and recommend alternate approaches that can lead to more cost-effective designs.

Of course, sound design is only the start. Execution of that design involves a long series of specialized steps including cutting, punching, forming, welding, grinding, finishing, and screen printing. Unlike most metalworking firms, however, Clark is equipped to do it all. As a sole-source supplier for its customers' metalworking needs, the company assumes full responsibility for its products from design through delivery. A full-time quality assurance department ensures that the company's rigorous ISO 9002 compliant standards are upheld throughout the entire process.

More than 100 trained technicians, together with an arsenal of highly versatile, computer-numerically-controlled machinery, give CMP exceptional capabilities. Executing production runs of widely different sizes, rapid changeover between jobs without retooling, and maintaining high levels of productivity despite short lead times have all been basic to the company's growth in the highly competitive precision sheet metal fabrication industry.

Sound principles of design, production, and delivery have made Clark Metal Products a trusted name among sophisticated equipment makers throughout the mid-Atlantic region.

While metalwork has always been at the core of Clark's business, making components for other companies wasn't the way it began. When J. W. Clark, Sr. opened his business in 1954, the company manufactured mailboxes, lawn furniture, and other metal products, which he marketed under the Clark name. Around 1960, as the market evolved, CMP transitioned into a job shop—a company that does subcontract work for others. Today, as a result, the company's products carry its customers' names rather than its own.

However, according to Jack Clark, Jr., president of Clark Metal Products and son of the company's founder, the satisfaction of being an integral part of the region's most advanced technology products more than offsets the "behind-the-scenes" quality of Clark's critical role. **Pa**

Center for Economic Operations of Indiana County

Expanding a business or creating a new one can be a daunting proposition almost anywhere. But in Indiana County, the Center for Economic Operations (CEO), which describes itself as a full- service business development agency, is making that task a little easier.

The CEO was created in 1994 to address the unmet needs of Indiana County's business community, according to its chief executive, Thomas Bayuzik. Until that time, there had been no organization with overall responsibility for assisting established businesses in the county. In addition, the unemployment resulting from a long decline in the county's once-powerful coal mining industry had also hurt the local economy. The CEO was formed to address both issues.

As a public/private partnership representing a variety of economic development organizations, the CEO pulls together all the elements of economic development under a single umbrella. Its members include Indiana County's Board of Commissioners, the Indiana County Chamber of Commerce, the Indiana County Development Corporation, the Indiana County Tourist Bureau, and the Indiana University of Pennsylvania.

As the initial point of contact for a variety of local resources and business assistance programs, the CEO offers help in a number of ways. For example, a new business seeking a home in Indiana County can consult the CEO for assistance in writing a business plan. The company will then be put in touch with personnel from Indiana University of Pennsylvania who specialize in that service.

Between 1994 and 1996, more than $20 million in economic and community development grants were secured through efforts of the CEO. Another $18 million in CEO-assisted direct business

Indiana University of Pennsylvania is home to the Corporate Campus business incubator, offering businesses the chance to achieve growth in an atmosphere of new ideas, entrepreneurial innovation, access to markets, ease of site selection, favorable financing, quality nearby amenities, and so much more.

loans are expected to create more than 1,000 jobs within the next five years in Indiana County. A majority of these jobs will be created at the new Indiana County Corporate Campus Business Park, a fully served 100-acre park, and the new Interchange Center, a 30,000-square-foot multi-tenant/business incubator facility. Located in Blairsville, Pennsylvania, these projects have immediate access to US Routes 22 and 119.

The success of the CEO public/private

Continued growth is a sign of strength at the new Interchange Center, a multi-tenant facility with space for all types of businesses, located at the heart of the Corporate Campus. The Interchange Center is ready for occupancy.

partnership results from matching and then applying the strengths of each member organization to the concerns of their various client businesses. "By putting our collective heads together, we do a much better job than if each of us were working independently," Mr. Bayuzik notes.

Among the coordination and referral services provided by the CEO are:

* Capital resources—helping businesses to find financing and providing information on tax incentives for new and existing businesses.

* Labor force readiness and training—preparing the county's work force to meet the needs of local industries while assisting businesses in locating qualified employees.

* Technology and communication resources—ensuring clients access to the latest telecommunication services and information networks.

* Site assistance—helping businesses locate ideal buildings and industrial sites and assisting industrial property owners in marketing their land and buildings.

* Utilities and transportation networks—providing information on water and sewage systems, transportation networks, and other infrastructure issues that businesses face.

* Information clearinghouse—providing information on the quality of life in Indiana County including community business profiles and business information kits.

By combining the strengths of its private and public sectors, the CEO works to revitalize the economy of Indiana County. Proving that its efforts are paying off, the work of the CEO was a compelling reason why the Pennsylvania Chamber of Business and Industry named Indiana County its "Outstanding Pennsylvania Community 1997." 🅿

Photo by Kevin Cooke/Graule Studios

Lawrence County

"Don't give up the ship!" Those dying words of American Navy Captain James Lawrence, delivered as his ship was bombarded by a British frigate, became a rallying cry of the War of 1812.

Three decades later, that phrase probably served as a rallying cry for civic and business leaders in the town of New Castle, already the leading commercial center of the area, in a geo-political battle they were waging. Then the boundary dividing Beaver and Mercer counties ran right through the town, splitting it and thoroughly complicating business and legal transactions. Against stiff political opposition, the leaders fought to have the boundary moved. In March 1849, the Pennsylvania Legislature responded, not by merely moving the boundary but by taking portions of Beaver and Mercer counties and creating a new county. Fittingly, New Castle, at the geographic center of the new county, was made county seat. Also fittingly, the new county was named in honor of Captain James Lawrence.

"Don't give up the ship" could well be Lawrence County's rallying cry today, as its people and its civic and business leaders work to revitalize the area and its economy.

Visitors are drawn to the picturesque historical sites found in villages such as Volant and New Wilmington. Photo by Kevin Cooke/Graule Studios

Their efforts and persistence are paying off. Since economic development became a priority in the county early in this decade and the private, non-profit Lawrence County Economic Development Corporation was established, nearly a thousand new jobs have been created, about four hundred jobs that were in jeopardy of moving have stayed, and development projects have attracted nearly $4 million in public funding—not insignificant results for a county that is the region's smallest in area and ranks seventh of ten in population.

Not only is heavy and light manufacturing making a comeback, but service-sector employment also is on the rise. Well-paying insurance-industry jobs are coming on line regularly. One of ten telephone call relay centers in the country, which handles 800-number calls from throughout the United States, has brought 150 new jobs to the county. That number is expected to double within a few years.

New businesses and new jobs are being attracted, and established employers not only are staying but many are expanding. There are good reasons why.

The county is affordable (commercial real estate costs are about a third of those in Pittsburgh, for example, and land in the county's eight publicly and privately owned industrial parks is available for as low as $7,500 an acre) and accessible (major highways serving the county include U.S. routes 422 and 224, state Route 18, the Pennsylvania Turnpike's Route 60, and three interstate highways: 76, 79, and 80).

Also, manufacturers locating in the county's Enterprise Zones in New Castle and Ellwood City are eligible for state economic incentives.

And employers find a willing, capable, and increasingly better educated labor pool from which to draw. Educational opportunities are both numerous and of high caliber. Lawrence Countians live no farther than twenty miles from nine college and university campuses, Westminster College in New Wilmington is very a very highly regarded liberal arts school, Pittsburgh's larger schools are just forty-five miles from New Castle, and there are numerous vocational training programs.

One of every four jobs in the county these days is in the service sector and more than half of them are in health care—the highest such percentage in the region. Manufacturing accounts for about 19 percent of all jobs.

One of the county's strengths is job diversity. Years ago, long before the rest of the region did so, Lawrence County diversified its economic base, which had been dominated by iron and steel. Lawrence acted in 1913, after a flood destroyed many of the area's riverside steel mills. The diversification was successful and the county was virtually alone in the region in missing the worst of the economic fallout from the steel industry's 1980s decline. Because manufacturers of chinaware, machinery,

Two sects of Old Order Amish have lived and farmed in Lawrence County for generations. Photo by Kevin Cooke/Graule Studios

controls, and other products continued doing well during that time, the county was able to maintain both higher living standards and employment rates than their neighbors.

A stubbornly sluggish national economy eventually caught up with the industries that were Lawrence County's economic mainstays. About ten years after hard times had hit the rest of the Pittsburgh region, they hit Lawrence. Some long-established plants closed, costing thousands of jobs. The county, accustomed to decades of virtually uninterrupted prosperity, found itself in failing economic health. Economic development became the county's top priority.

Local observers are hardly surprised by the effort's recent successes. They know the county's long and impressive history.

The area that eventually became Lawrence County, situated around the confluence of Shenanago, Mahoning, and Beaver rivers, long had been a favored Indian trading place because it was easily accessible from many directions by canoe. Settlers began moving into the area late in the 18th century.

The rivers attracted settlers and such natural resources as coal, iron ore, clay, and limestone attracted and encouraged industrial development. One of the first structures erected in what is now New Castle was a small iron forge built on the banks of Neshannock Creek. Canals also played a role. The north-to-south Beaver and Erie Canal that linked Pittsburgh with Lake Erie ran through New Castle, and the Pennsylvania and Ohio Canal bisected the county east to west.

The iron industry flourished from 1840 until after the Civil War. During the 1840s, a carding works, bolt and nut factory, furniture factory, and glass works all began operating in the area. Thomas McConnell's mill, built in 1868, was one of the first rolling mills in the United States. It processed corn, oats, wheat, and buckwheat. (The site is now McConnell's Mill State Park, one of the state's most spectacular sights.)

Agricultural and dairy products were important segments of Lawrence County's early economy, as were chemicals and allied products, leather goods, and lumber. By 1890, industrial growth surged and the steel industry began its

tremendous early growth. In 1893, the county's first tinplate mill began operating and it was not many years before New Castle became the Tinplate Capital of the World. The first piece of seamless pipe made in the United States was produced at Ellwood City in 1895. Shenango China Company began production and soon was the largest manufacturer of vitrified china in the world. New Castle became one of the largest manufacturers of chinaware in the country.

The start of a new century saw the beginnings of a new industry in the county: fireworks manufacturing. Before long, more fireworks were being made in Lawrence County than anywhere else in the United States. That allowed New Castle, still home to two fireworks makers, to call itself the Fireworks Capital of America—a title it still claims. The city annually hosts a colorful and loud fireworks festival that attracts thousands.

New Castle could claim to have been home to the world's first multiple-screen movie theater, one owned by the Warner Brothers before their Hollywood fame. Brothers Albert and Sam Warner from nearby Youngstown, Ohio, traveled throughout the area with a copy of *The Great Train Robbery* and eventually settled in New Castle. They rented a second-floor room on South Mill Street and borrowed ninety-nine chairs from a funeral home. Shortly afterward, they moved to the ground floor, bought their own chairs, and opened their primitive "multiplex": three rooms where three different short films were shown.

The Warners' theater attracted crowds back then. The county's many crowd-appealing attractions are doing the same today on a much grander scale. Tourism

Tourism is an important part of Lawrence County's economy, with two big draws being McConnell's Mill State Park and Moraine State Park, as well as the numerous streams and rivers found throughout the county that are prized for boating and fishing. Photo by Kevin Cooke/Graule Studios

is becoming a major player in Lawrence's economy. McConnell's Mill State Park and Moraine State Park, with its 3,000-acre lake, are big draws, as are the numerous streams and rivers that are prized for boating and fishing. Many visitors come to shop for goods produced by the two sects of Old Order Amish people who have lived and farmed in the county for generations and whose horse-drawn buggies are rather familiar sights, even on some of the county's busiest roads. Sightseers and shoppers crowd the streets of the county's small villages like Volant and New Wilmington. Other attractions include the Scottish Rite Cathedral in New Castle, which has one of the largest performance stages east of the Mississippi River, and the county's several covered bridges.

Lawrence County is working hard to attract visitors with money to spend. It is working even harder to attract new businesses with jobs to provide, while keeping established businesses and helping them grow.

As part of that effort, the Lawrence County Economic Development Corporation is focusing on developing industrial and commercial sites in the county. It has completed the infrastructure for Shenango Commerce Park, a 40-acre site it owns along the Shenango River; is erecting two buildings at New Castle Commerce Park, which is owned by the city of New Castle; and is assisting in the ongoing development of the R.J. Casey Industrial Park owned by the borough of Ellwood City and River View Commerce Park, a publicly-owned park in New Castle. The LCEDC also works with the owners of the county's four private parks in Wampum Borough and Shenango, Neshannock, and North Beaver townships.

And the New Castle Sanitation Authority, in an effort to encourage economic development projects in its service area, is almost doubling the capacity of its processing plant.

Planning is critical to the success of these and similar public and private efforts designed to revitalize Lawrence County and its economy. The county Chamber of Commerce, working with the Pennsylvania Economy League, is leading the effort to implement a county strategic plan covering economic development, tourism, housing, planning, and government.

The plan realistically addresses nuts-and-bolts issues and concerns. Its framers are confident it will provide a reliable structure for implementing revitalization efforts. They are equally confident that it will succeed because its success depends

Sightseers and shoppers enjoy a visit to the village of Volant, where they can enjoy unique stores and restaurants. Photo by Kevin Cooke/Graule Studios

ultimately upon the support of the people of Lawrence County, who are proud of their history and eager once again to show the world that that history certainly can repeat itself. 𝗣𝗮

WASHINGTON

1711

Washington County

There are hundreds of places throughout the United States named in honor of our nation's first president. But it is unlikely that any of them has a more legitimate claim of close association with George Washington than Washington County. George not only undoubtedly slept there, he owned more than 2,800 acres of land there—land he bought two years before the start of the Revolutionary War. He even, while serving as president in 1794, personally led a company of militia against farmers in the area who had rebelled against the government's imposition of an excise tax on whiskey, which the farmers produced and counted on for a substantial portion of their income. No U.S. president since has led troops into battle, if a confrontation between a largely unorganized group of farmers and approximately thirteen thousand militiamen recruited from four states could be considered much of a battle.

Historians regard the Whiskey Rebellion as the first test of the power of the fledgling federal government. In suppressing it, President Washington firmly established the federal government's primacy in disputes with individual states. And although frontier farmers from throughout southwestern Pennsylvania participated in the insurrection (the tarring and feathering of tax collectors being a particularly popular form of participation), many of its most noted and notorious events took place in Washington County.

Several sites associated with the uprising serve today as tourist attractions. They include David Bradford House, the elegant home in Little Washington (as the county seat is so frequently referred to in a highly successful effort to avoid confusing it with the nation's capital) of one of the rebellion's top leaders. Others include Ginger Hill and Whiskey Point near Monongahela, where the insurgents gathered.

By imposing the whiskey tax in the first place and by taking such an active role as a militia leader in suppressing the rebellion in the second, President

Washington County is home to the Trolley Museum, which is dedicated to preserving historic rail cars to be enjoyed by visitors from throughout the region. Photo by Kevin Cooke/Graule Studios

The county was named for George Washington, first President of the United States, who was a landowner here. Photo by Kevin Cooke/Graule Studios

Washington became a very unpopular person throughout Southwestern Pennsylvania at the time, especially in Washington County. He was a neighbor who owned land in the county, after all, so he had to have known how economically important whiskey and whiskey making was to the farmers. The feeling was that he should have shown some compassion to them and their cause.

George Washington's unpopularity among Washington Countians in 1794 contrasted sharply with his overwhelming popularity there thirteen years earlier. Then, in 1781, two years before the Treaty of Paris ended the Revolutionary War, he was widely and wildly acclaimed as a hero, a bold and resourceful military leader. It is hardly surprising that the new county established that year should honor him by taking his name.

Organized out of Westmoreland County, Washington County originally included all of Greene and Beaver counties and a large part of Allegheny County. (Now with 863 square miles, it is the second largest county in the region and is the third most populous.) Most of its early settlers arrived from Virginia by way of the Monongahela River, Ten Mile Creek, and Whiteley Creek.

Early on, the Mon River was the county's principal transportation resource. Its role was hardly diminished by the opening of the National Road (now U.S. Route 40). Created by an 1806 Act of Congress as the first federally supported roadway, the National Road from Cumberland, Maryland, to Wheeling, West Virginia, for decades was the nation's busiest land artery to the west. Today, it still serves as a critically important—and tremendously scenic—passageway through the county. (Its historical and economic importance has been celebrated for the past twenty-five years with the National Road Festival, featuring events along its entire 90-mile length in Washington and neighboring Fayette County.) Today, the National Road, Interstate 70 and its link to the Pennsylvania Turnpike, I79, U.S. Routes 19 and 22, and state Routes 50 and 88 comprise the county's vital highway network.

The National Road played a key role in Washington's early development and helped move the goods and materials to and from the county's burgeoning

Employment in manufacturing is increasing in Washington County, and now accounts for more than 20 percent of the county's jobs. Photo by Kevin Cooke/Graule Studios

industries. The glass industry was established after the Civil War and some of the finest glassware in the country was produced in Little Washington and Charleroi. Canonsburg became noted for producing pottery, china, and tinplate and ternplate. Oil and natural gas discoveries led to both economic and population growth.

But it was coal that fueled the county's development. Rich deposits of coal were discovered before 1800 near Canonsburg and Washington. It was not long before coal mining became the largest industry in the county.

Coal was not the only industry offering jobs and paychecks, of course. Steel mills lined the banks of the Monongahela; Donora became one of the largest manufacturers of steel wire in world. The now defunct Standard Industries in Canonsburg was one of the world's largest early producers of radium.

Despite its ranking as the third most populous county in the region, Washington County is largely rural with a full range of rural amenities. There still

are twenty-three preserved covered bridges in the county, most of them over 100 years old. (Washington and neighboring Greene County jointly hold a Covered Bridge Festival each September.) Meadowcroft Museum of Rural Life near Avella is a 200-acre outdoor museum of life on the land in western Pennsylvania. And the county is home to about sixteen hundred farms producing mainly milk and dairy products.

The county may be rural but job opportunities have a decided urban flavor. Today, about one of every four jobs in the county is in the service sector, with about 40 percent of them in health care. Employment in manufacturing, particularly of primary and fabricated metals, glass, plastic, paper, and electronics as well as in machine shop operations, has increased recently. Manufacturing now accounts for about 20 percent of the county's jobs.

Economic development officials identify electronics, metals fabrication, machining, plastics, information technologies, and retailing (with two new shopping malls under construction and another undergoing major expansion) as the county's fastest growing employment categories.

Those officials also say that the county is suffering from shortage of skilled metal workers. And there is heavy

demand for computer literate office technology/business application workers, health care givers, and such high-end professionals as engineers, management information systems experts, and accounting and marketing people.

Those demands and shortages are the direct result of an ambitious economic development effort led by elected officials, the county's Redevelopment Authority and the Washington County Council on Economic Development, among others. Through the efforts of several agencies, thirty-six new companies have been attracted to the county, a number of companies that were in danger of closing or leaving have stayed, and some twenty-five hundred new, well paying jobs have been added over the past five years.

The county has a lot to offer companies considering moving into Washington and resident firms seeking to grow and expand: low taxes, utility, and land costs, and the presence of a stable, reliable, and capable work force. The county's educational institutions also play a key role. Quality business and career training is offered by Washington & Jefferson College and California University of Pennsylvania, backed by two public vocational-technical schools and six private trade and vocational schools. W&J, California, and the University of Pittsburgh also offer budding entrepreneurs free-of-charge help in drafting business plans.

Another key element of Washington County's job-creation, business-attraction formula has been the development of industrial/manufacturing/office/technology parks. There are twenty such parks operating now, eight of them publicly owned. Very few vacancies exist in the parks and several are at full capacity.

The most successful such park is Southpointe on Interstate 79 in Cecil Township, not far from the Allegheny County border. Southpointe has been called one of the top five office park developments in the northeastern United States. Less than six years into its active development, the 573-acre mixed-use park (besides office and manufacturing buildings it also has a golf course and high-end residential units) has run out of vacant land to lease. When all construction is completed, employment at Southpointe is expected to reach at least twenty-eight hundred.

Southpointe's success probably would not have been so complete and so swift without the cordial working relationship that has been established between county officials and developers. Developers working at Southpointe and at other parks in the county say the county commissioners, the Redevelopment Authority, and other agencies are both receptive and very cooperative. Southpointe by definition is a public-pri-

The county is home to about sixteen hundred farms producing mainly milk and dairy products. Photo by Kevin Cooke/Graule Studios

vate partnership, they point out, and has been run that way. One developer has been quoted as saying that the entire region needs more partnership arrangements like Southpointe if revitalization hopes are to be realized.

Southpointe has proven to be so successful in so short a time that county officials are eager to develop a clone, preferably in the northwestern part of the county near U.S. Route 22 and even closer to Pittsburgh's downtown than Southpointe.

As much as they need more business and mixed-use parks to bolster their economic revitalization efforts, county officials say they need road improvements even more. Recent progress has moved two proposed and long-discussed highways that are critical to the county's future economic well being further along in the planning process and closer to final approval: the Southern Beltway and the Mon-Fayette Expressway. County leaders have been talking about the

expressway for almost thirty years and touting it as a critical element in efforts to revive the economies not only of Washington and neighboring southern counties but also the old steel towns in southeastern Allegheny County.

Completion of those high-speed, limited-access highways will open sizable areas of the county to development and provide county residents and businesses with quicker and easier access not only to the City of Pittsburgh and Pittsburgh International Airport to the north, but also to locations—and markets—to the south.

Given all else that Washington County has to offer, the new highways will give the county one of the strongest and most complete business and job attraction packages in the region. 🅿️

Chapter

11

Westmoreland County

I t's the biggest county in the region in area (1,033 square miles) and at one time included all of what are now Greene, Fayette, and Washington counties and parts of Allegheny, Armstrong, Beaver, and Indiana counties as well. It was the first English-speaking county in the country west of the Allegheny Mountains when it was established in 1773. It's the region's second most populous after Allegheny County—and it's growing. And at a time when many economies are dominated by start-up service companies with strange-sounding names, half of its list of twenty-four largest employers are industrial firms with familiar names and established reputations.

In one recent two-year period, thirty-six new companies moved into the county (most of them industrial firms) and forty already-established companies expanded their operations and their payrolls. Together, the new arrivals and the growing resident firms created about twenty-five hundred new jobs. In that period, other jobs—estimated at a couple thousand at least—did not leave the county when employers became convinced that they were better off continuing to operate in the county than moving to what may have seemed like greener pastures elsewhere.

As far as local government, civic, business, and economic leaders are concerned, there are no greener pastures in the Pittsburgh region than those found in Westmoreland County. And they work as hard to keep the companies they have as they do in luring new firms to set up shop there.

There are a number of things that contribute to the bright green glow of Westmoreland's pastures. For example, the Westmoreland County Airport in Latrobe is the only airport in the region besides Pittsburgh International with daily passenger service. (A $4.75 million project will extend the airport's runways

and expand the terminal and should help attract additional airlines and more passenger and freight service.) The county has an extensive public and private industrial park system that is the envy of the region. Also enviable are electric utility rates that are below the national average, a reliable supply of competitively priced natural gas (thanks to the presence in the county of one of the country's largest natural gas storage facilities), low taxes, a skilled and educated labor pool, and good access to major interstate highways and the markets they serve.

And speaking of market access, Westmoreland businesses have more of it since the Westmoreland County Industrial Development Corporation, the county's principal economic develop-

ment agency, acquired and subsequently rehabilitated thirty-eight miles of track in the central and south central sections of the county and merged it with an adjoining line in neighboring Fayette County to form a 65-mile-long system called the Southwest Pennsylvania Railroad. The line links businesses in both counties with large rail carriers and the markets they serve and contributed to a decision by at least one large manufacturer to move into Westmoreland.

Couple all that with quality-of-life factors that attract and keep new residents: the opportunity to live in a small-town atmosphere that is mostly fields and woodlands yet is only a 45-minute drive to a major economic and cultural center; with eight county parks, two state parks, and thirty-one golf courses; with numerous art and theater venues and annual host of the third largest arts festival in Pennsylvania; with plentiful facilities for skiing, biking, hiking, fishing, hunting, boating, canoeing, spelunking, and camping; and that has the lowest crime rate of the ten Pennsylvania counties with 300,000 or more people.

Westmoreland is the biggest county in the region in area, and offers plentiful land and facilities for skiing, biking, hiking, fishing, hunting, boating, canoeing, spelunking, camping, and a wide variety of other outdoor activities—all within a 45-minute drive to the major economic and cultural center of the City of Pittsburgh. Photos by Kevin Cooke/Graule Studios

It is hardly surprising that Westmoreland's population is projected to grow to more than 400,000 from the current level of about 377,000 by the time the next U.S. Census is tallied.

Westmoreland residents are an increasingly well-educated bunch. Almost three out of every four county high school graduates go on to college. More than 15 percent of them hold bachelors degrees and above. The percentage of high school and college graduates in the county is higher than the state's average and there currently are more than 11,300 students enrolled in Westmoreland's institutions of higher learning: St. Vincent College, Seton Hill College, University of Pittsburgh at Greensburg, Penn State-New Kensington, and Community College of Westmoreland County.

Those institutions and the county's vocational, technical, and trade schools as well as the educational opportunities

available in not-too-far-away Pittsburgh are preparing residents to take their places as members of an increasingly well educated, skilled, and trained workforce that employers are very eager to tap. Currently, most (about 64 percent) Westmoreland residents have jobs in the county. About one of every four residents is employed by service providers, with more than 40 percent of those engaged in health care, primarily in the county's four major hospitals in Greensburg, Latrobe, Jeannette, and New Kensington. Retailing is the next largest employment category, while manufacturing places a solid third and is growing.

Manufacturing's revival is a welcome sign to those who remember fondly Westmoreland's industrial history and heritage—that not-so-long-ago past when the city of New Kensington was one of the most extensive producers of aluminum in the world, when Arnold and Jeannette had large window-glass plants, when Mount Pleasant and Grapeville were noted for glass manufacturing, when Latrobe was known as the tool steel capital and manufactured some of the world's largest casting molds, and

when Monessen (named for the German steel making city of Essen, thus Essen on the Monongahela—or Mon—River), was one of the world's premier steel producers.

The county's industrial roots go back much further than that. The area's earliest industrial enterprises produced iron (the Westmoreland Furnace, only the third stone blast furnace built west of the Allegheny Mountains, was one of sixteen in the county), coke, bituminous coal, salt, glass, and natural gas.

Westmoreland later gained fame as the site of the first auto assembly plant in the United States operated by a foreign auto maker when Volkswagen started producing Rabbits near New Stanton in the mid-1970s.

Other Westmoreland "firsts": The world's first suspension bridge was built over Jacob's Creek near Greensburg in 1796; it was 70 feet long and cost $6,000. Latrobe claims to have been the site of the world's first professional football game on September 3, 1895, for which one player was paid $10 and expenses. That is a disputed "first," but no one doubts that the world's first banana split was created in a Latrobe drugstore in 1904.

Since Westmoreland was the first English speaking county established west of the Alleghenies, it follows that its first capital, Hanna's Town (not to be confused with Hannastown, a nearby mining town) was the first county seat west of those mountains. After Hanna's Town was sacked and burned by Indians, the county seat was moved to Greensburg.

Today Greensburg serves as the nerve center for the county's

Westmoreland county boasts eight county parks, two state parks, and thirty-one golf courses, along with art and theater venues, and the third largest arts festival in Pennsylvania. Photo by Kevin Cooke/Graule Studios

economic revitalization efforts that have achieved rather remarkable results. Much of their success can be attributed to the county's multi-industrial park system: nine publicly operated parks, with two more proposed, and twenty privately owned and operated parks throughout the county with land and buildings available at what officials call very reasonable rates.

The county's economic development professionals have a reputation for proactive marketing and for paying as much attention to the smallest resident company or prospect as they do large multi-nationals. What sets Westmoreland apart from some counties is a full-service approach. The Westmoreland development team wraps everything a prospect needs into one neat package: land, facility, infrastructure, permits, and financing. It's an approach that prevents permitting and construction delays and knocks valuable time off project schedules.

As heartening as their success at attracting and keeping employers has

been, development and local and county government leaders are not resting on their laurels. They are continuing to devise and implement strategies to maintain and increase development momentum.

High among their priorities are infrastructure improvements. Although the county is reasonably well served by its highway system (featuring Interstate 76—the Pennsylvania Turnpike,

Among the many special microbrewed beers in the region is Eureka Gold Crown Beer, made by the Jones Brewing Company, est. 1909, better known as "Stoney's Beer." According to the local stories, the beer was first brewed by Stoney Jones, who gave it its original regal name. But the large immigrant population of the area at the time found the long name difficult to pronounce, so they would enter their local pub and ask simply for "one of Stoney's beers." The nickname stuck, and today the Jones Brewing Company still produces "Stoney's." Photo by Kevin Cooke/Graule   Studios

Manufacturing is experiencing a revival in the county, a welcome sign to those who fondly remember Westmoreland's proud industrial history and heritage. Photo by Kevin Cooke/Graule   Studios

The world's first banana split was created in Westmoreland County in 1904, in
a Latrobe drugstore. Today, Joe Greubel,
president of the Valley Dairy in Latrobe,
is proud to recreate the confection
according to its "original formula."
Photo by Kevin Cooke/Graule Studios

To assure Westmoreland's continued growth, county leaders are working to extend a U.S. 22 upgrade project, and hope to construct three new expressways, making it easier to commute to and from the county. Photo by Kevin Cooke/Graule Studios

Interstate 70, U.S. Routes 22, 30, and 119, and the Amos K. Hutchinson Bypass—a limited-access road linking Route 22 at Delmont with the Turnpike at New Stanton), improvements are sorely needed. County leaders are seeking to extend an already extensive U.S. Route 22 upgrading project. Among the items on their infrastructure "wish list" is the construction of three expressways: the $150 million Laurel Valley Expressway to link the county airport to Interstates 76 and 70 at New Stanton (and which would provide access to newly available industrial park sites); the Kiski Valley Expressway to link Vandergrift and the

Allegheny Valley Expressway (and cut dramatically travel time from the northwestern corner of the county to Pittsburgh); and the New Kensington Expressway to improve access to industrial sites in New Kensington and Arnold.

Westmoreland's growth strategy also relies heavily on continuing development of the industrial park system. In the works or on the drawing boards are park expansions and additions that, when coupled with redevelopment projects at old industrial sites and other construction and site renewal efforts, could attract another 11,000 or more new jobs to Westmoreland.

In the fall of 1996 Westmoreland County had erected a huge billboard on some highways leading into downtown Pittsburgh. It carried the message, "Westmoreland County ... the smart choice for your business expansion" and listed the reasons why: low taxes and

utilities, fully developed sites, skilled workforce, low crime rate, and high quality of life. Some development officials saw the sign as a blatant attempt to steal business from Pittsburgh and were offended. No offense intended, their Westmoreland counterparts insisted. It was, they said, merely part of their overall marketing effort and their way of touting their county's obvious advantages. It also could be seen as a challenge to the other counties to develop the type of progressive strategies that have helped Westmoreland achieve a level of economic revitalization and job creation success that, were it widely duplicated, could appreciably shorten the time it will take for the Pittsburgh region to regain its status as an economic and industrial powerhouse. **Pa**

Sony Technology Center-Pittsburgh

W hen Sony began searching for a new Eastern U.S. site to build its large-screen TV sets during the late 1980s, the company had its pick of virtually any location in the country. But what Sony wanted — in a workforce, in a plant site and in proximity to its markets — it found at Mount Pleasant, Pennsylvania. In 1990, Sony officially took over the site of an old auto assembly plant and began to develop its technology center. The 650-acre campus is located near two major interstate highways, and is within two days' drive of more than 60 percent of Sony's North American markets.

Since its conception, the site has become the world's first vertically integrated television manufacturing site. It is the only

At the Sony Technology Center-Pittsburgh, the American Video Glass Company's state-of-the-art manufacturing facility is located across the street from one of its customer's largest production facilities.

facility capable of going from sand to glass to television picture tube to finished television set — all in one location.

The site, known as the Sony Technology Center-Pittsburgh, employs approximately 3,000 on site. Sony's impact on the local economy has not stopped at the plant gates. The facility contracts for parts, materials, services, and equipment with more than 1,100 local suppliers in the immediate area.

Sony Electronics Inc.

Since production began in July of 1992 with large-screen rear projection televi-

The Sony building in Mount Pleasant is home to Sony Electronics Inc. and Sony Chemicals Corporation of America.

sion sets, the Technology Center has expanded its capabilities and products. The site has become the global engineering center for large-screen rear projection television sets. It is the only location to produce Sony's 32- and 36-inch FD Trinitron® television sets, featuring a flat-screened picture tube, and Sony's 35-inch Trinitron TV.

In addition, the plant produces Videoscope® rear projection sets with

screen sizes ranging from 41 to 61 inches. It also manufactures the 7-inch color television picture tubes used in the projection sets.

Three years after production began, Sony added another essential element to its production at Mount Pleasant. Aperture grilles—a key component of a Trinitron television picture tube—went into production in 1995. This expansion gave Sony its first in-house production capability for this essential component, and the site supplies Sony plants in San Diego, the United Kingdom, Singapore, and Japan, as well as the picture tube production in Mount Pleasant.

Coupled with the expanded production has come an increasing emphasis on procuring parts locally. For example, nearly 100 percent of the mechanical parts used in Sony's projection TV sets come from sources within 300 miles of the plant. Altogether, nearly 90 percent of the material used in the Sony's projection TV sets comes from suppliers based in the United States. And of that group, most are rooted in southwestern Pennsylvania.

North America's large numbers of television households constitute the pri-

Picture tubes for the FD Trinitron® Wega television are in production. The tube uses a perfectly flat screen to eliminate distortion caused by curvature. Pittsburgh is the only facility outside Japan to build flat picture tubes and television sets.

A Sony Company Member conducts the final inspection on a Sony Videoscope® television set. Each person involved in the manufacturing process can reject any set that does not meet Sony's high quality standards.

mary market for TV sets produced at Mount Pleasant. Sony also exports to overseas markets, and produces these smaller volume orders in crew cells — teams of self-directed workers — rather than on the main production line. Each crew cell builds a set from start to finish, and the approach allows for a high degree of flexibility in the production process.

In keeping with Sony's original vision of building a manufacturing organization with true vertical integration, as its television assembly operation grew, Mount Pleasant also became home to the American Video Glass Company and the Sony Chemicals Corporation of America, a separate unit of Sony Corporation. Through the late 1990s, Sony's investment is in excess of a half-billion dollars, with plans for future expansion.

American Video Glass Company

November 1995 witnessed the groundbreaking at the Sony Technology Center for a new $300 million plant created by a unique partnership between Sony Electronics Inc. and Corning Asahi Video Products. The partnership, named the American Video Glass Company, is devoted solely to producing the high-quality glass used in Sony's television picture tubes.

The decision to locate the partnership's glass-making facility at Mount Pleasant was driven in part by Sony's desire to develop a single-site vertically integrated television manufacturing operation. But in the case of American Video, there were other factors that influenced the decision. The region's history of glass-making means many members of the facility's highly-skilled workforce bring industry-specific experience with them.

The plant's utility costs are among the lowest in the industry. Raw materials, which are delivered primarily by bulk rail cars, are readily available from nearby suppliers. American Video also has a sister Corning Asahi glass-making plant in State College, about 120 miles away. The State College facility was instrumental in the start-up of American Video, and the company has continued to benefit from its sister plant's experiences.

Because the high-temperature melting furnaces must run nonstop throughout the year, American Video operates on a 24-hours-a-day, seven-days-a-week schedule. Approximately 550 employees keep the 750,000-square-foot plant operating. Every day, nearly 500 tons of silica sand and other raw materials are made into molten glass, which is then formed into "gobs" that are dropped into molds and pressed into the shape of television picture tube panels and funnels — the glass components that form the cathode ray

American Video robots automatically unload funnels from the annealing lehr (oven).

tube. Once the glass has cooled, the panels — which will become the viewing area of a television set — are polished into an optically flawless viewing surface.

Once they are formed and polished, the glass parts are shipped off to another Sony manufacturing facility to be made into television picture tubes. For the company's popular 27- and 32-inch sets, the destination is Sony's San Diego facility. For the new flat 32-inch FD Trinitrons, the glass need only move across the street to Sony's cathode ray tube operation.

Altogether, the American Video facility has the capability to deliver more than four million pieces of finished glass to Sony's picture tube manufacturing plants every year.

Sony Chemicals Corporation of America

The same year that ground was broken for the American Video Glass plant, an altogether different Sony operation was begun at the Technology Center. Sony Chemicals Corporation of America opened its first North American manufacturing facility on the site in 1995. The company produces coated thermal transfer ribbon used in manufacturing, inventory control, logistics, and distribu-

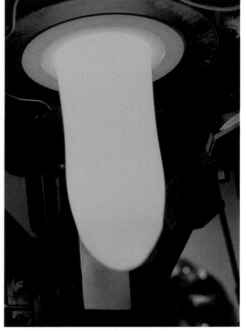

Each day, American Video feeds nearly 20,000 gobs of molten glass, as seen here, into its panel and funnel forming processes.

tion along with a variety of industrial adhesives.

The primary application of the plant's thermal transfer ribbon is for bar coding. Clear plastic ribbon, with its bar code marked in ink to show the appropriate size and feature information, is fused with heat onto components, as well as onto finished products and product packaging. At key points throughout the manufacturing and distribution process, high-speed computer scanners read the codes to track and control the movement of the labeled materials.

Although most of the ribbon is removed before the products reach their end users, a growing number of consumer applications have also been developed using thermal transfer ribbon technology. The size markings that appear on Levi jeans in clothing store shelves, for example, are printed onto thermal transfer ribbon made at Mount Pleasant. So is the identification information used by many states on hunting and driver's licenses.

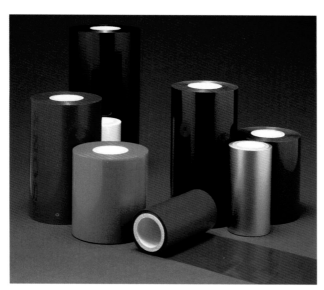

Sony Chemicals is recognized around the world for superior thermal transfer ribbon technologies that deliver performance and total cost advantages.

The proprietary binding and coating systems that form the technical building blocks of Sony Chemicals' thermal transfer ribbon products are also the focus of new product development at Mount Pleasant. As the company's headquarters site for all of North and South America, the Technology Center includes a comprehensive research and development lab, as well as production areas. The site also holds Sony Chemicals' quality control, applications engineering, and sales and marketing functions.

Adhesives produced by Sony Chemicals are particularly well suited to difficult bonding and exacting protective coating applications. For example, liquid adhesives and adhesive-coated tapes from Sony are frequently used in the consumer electronics, communications, automotive, and aeronautics industries. Sony Chemicals' special ultraviolet-curable coating provides performance and durability for customers facing demanding challenges in the manufacture of computer parts, television components, compact discs, and the new generation of digital video disc.

Sony Chemicals also produces a wide variety of industrial products including a broad line of advanced technology products.

Management and Community Philosophy

One of the most distinctive features of Sony's Mount Pleasant operation is the company's innovative management style. Its team approach to managing the workplace has earned the facility recognition by consultants Arthur D. Little, Inc. as one of America's top twenty companies in manufacturing management.

Every Sony group has teams operating within their own work areas. This management structure empowers the employees at every level to participate in making decisions that directly impact their work. For example, in the television assembly area, self-directed teams decide how many sets to manufacture each day to meet production targets, what parts to order, and how to staff the various functions. As a result, the facility's management structure is relatively flat, with every individual realizing their direct impact on costs and quality.

Sony believes that cooperation and teamwork extend beyond the workplace. Accordingly, the company is a leader in developing environmentally friendly methods of handling byproducts from its manufacturing processes. The approach used to handle the iron chloride waste that resulted from the production of aperture grilles is typical of Sony's philosophy.

Sony discovered that the iron chloride could be used to control pollutants in the waste stream by removing harmful

sediments. As a result, iron chloride generated at the facility is now being sold to a local water treatment facility where it is used to purify wastewater from sewage before that water is discharged into local rivers and streams. Both Sony Chemicals and Sony Electronics have earned ISO 9001 and 14001 certification as a result of their efforts. In keeping with the ISO 14001 protocol, Sony created a recyclable packaging design that substantially reduces waste in another area of its operation.

Outside the workplace, Sony has extended this participatory approach to include its surrounding community. The facility has adopted a local school, participates in PennDOT's "Adopt-a-Highway" program, and hosts educators and students for job-shadowing experiences where participants learn hands-on about careers in high tech manufacturing. Additionally, employees at every level of Sony are active in many non-profit organizations that serve their home communities. **Pa**

Sony Chemical's technical services laboratory is available for problem solving and product testing.

Robicon

Who controls the factory machines that spin agitators, power pumps, circulate air, move conveyors, and grind bulky materials into a pulp? For more than 30 years, in one industry after another, the answer has been Robicon—a western Pennsylvania maker of power conversion solutions serving industrial customers with installations in 57 countries around the world.

Since its startup in 1964 by former Westinghouse engineers, Robicon has expanded, relocated, and changed hands throughout the years. But through it all, converting electric power with high levels of precision and reliability has remained the company's exclusive focus. The reason is simple.

The process motors that drive factory equipment constitute the single largest source of electrical use in the United States today. The effectiveness, energy consumption, and lifespan of these costly motors and of the custom-built devices they operate are all directly linked to the dimensions of the electrical current that drives them. Controlling that power is a demanding assignment—one for which standard, off-the-shelf solutions are

Converting electric power with high levels of precision and reliability is Robicon's exclusive focus.

rarely good enough.

From their company's outset as a fledgling operation in Pittsburgh's East Liberty section, Robicon's founders understood the importance of tailoring conversion solutions to the specific demands of each customer and each job application. And as electrical engineers with extensive experience in solving problems for industry, they were determined to transform their professional skill into a core asset of the new business.

Custom engineering remains the foundation of Robicon's business. While competing companies often try to force their standard products onto customers, Robicon creates custom solutions in each of its major application areas. Today, as a result, more employees at Robicon are involved in design and application engineering than in any other function.

Those applications cover the full spectrum of industrial activity. Robicon solutions are routinely found in plants belonging to some of the world's largest mining, pipeline, environmental, and metals interests. Oil exploration companies, for example, are now drilling to previously unimagined depths and opening

Robicon produces power control systems, serving industrial customers with installations in 57 countries around the world.

up promising new reserves thanks to a new generation of electrical submersible pumps controlled by Robicon drives.

A 600-horsepower Robicon AC drive, which was recently installed into a t unnel in Brooklyn's Gowanus Canal, is now turning a propeller that draws 300 million gallons of water a day from New York Harbor into the nearby freight canal. After more than thirty-five years, a still-water stench and the nickname "perfume creek" are history.

All across the nation, large-scale mining operations, refineries, paper-making firms, transmission pipelines, and water treatment facilities have also joined the company's impressive roster of client industries.

Through the years, Robicon has built and marketed virtually every known configuration of power circuit for motor drives. Its track record as a producer of power supply equipment is equally impressive. And in 1989, when the firm merged with Halmar—then a leading maker of specialty silicon controlled rectifier power controls—the combined company could boast a larger base of installed SCR power controllers than any other manufacturer.

As it grew during the years, Robicon's operations were acquired, divested, and merged with a succession of larger technology firms. To accommodate that expansion, the company required ever-larger facilities. In 1968, the company moved from its original site in Pittsburgh to a new facility in Plum Boro—an eastern suburb of the city. Then in 1995, with the financial backing of its parent company—High Voltage Engineering Corporation—Robicon completed its newest facility in nearby New Kensington, which it now operates jointly with its Plum Boro plant.

Together, the company's two facilities encompass 200,000 square feet of work space. Of that area, a little more than half is devoted to its climate-controlled manufacturing and testing facilities. Dynomometer rooms, containing all of the motor and reactor loads used for testing, account for approximately 10,000 square feet. A separate 5,000-square-foot product research and development lab is also used for in-depth performance assessment and environmental testing of its custom power controls before they are shipped off to customers.

Robicon today is one of Pittsburgh's fastest-growing companies. In addition to

Robicon's two facilities, located in Plum Boro and New Kensington, Pennsylvania, encompass 200,000 square feet of work space.

the steady expansion of industrial markets at home and abroad, several factors distinctive to the electrical power business have been driving much of that growth. One is the ongoing deregulation and restructuring of the world's energy markets. Inefficiencies which may have been acceptable under regulated monopolies are simply intolerable in a competitive marketplace. As a result, a new generation of sophisticated power distribution and control equipment is making electric power a far more efficient source of energy than at any time in history.

Beyond that, a growing awareness of air quality issues, together with increasing political pressure to reduce the greenhouse gas emissions associated with power generation and use, are also exercising an influence. The requirements for power control and conversion equipment, as a consequence, are changing as well. So are the new, high-efficiency process motors they are being used to drive.

There is also a growing transmission problem resulting from the widespread introduction of computers. Any electronic device using solid state power switching to convert AC to DC disrupts the nor-

Custom engineering remains the foundation of Robicon's business.

mal linear flow of power both on the customer's own site and, in many instances, for other customers on the same power grid. Harmonics—unwanted multiples of the normal 60-cycle power line frequency—are introduced into the power distribution lines as the direct result of these devices. And those distortions create problems for other electric users including cross-talk, overload, poor voltage regulation and inefficient power consumption.

In the United States today, only about 20 percent of the electrical utility distribution load is non-linear. But within as little as a decade, that number could rise to 75 percent. Internationally, some countries are already ahead of this pace. To combat that pattern, the prestigious Institute of Electrical and Electronics Engineers issued a series of recommended power quality practices and requirements. Robicon soltuions allow users to meet exacting standards for current and voltage without having to invest in costly filters to correct harmonic distortion.

With Robicon technologies at work around the world, the future of electric power has never been under better control. **Pa**

Dormont Manufacturing Company

What do twenty thousand McDonalds restaurants have in common with London's House of Parliament and millions of private homes across the United States? It's that their cooking and heating appliances are all tied into gas lines with flexible stainless steel gas connectors made by Dormont Manufacturing Company—a world-class manufacturing operation in Westmoreland County that feels like a family business.

Dormont, which now dominates the U.S. residential and food service markets for gas line connectors, is growing faster than the industries it serves. With revenues expanding at an annual rate of 20 percent and an ambitious program of new product introductions now underway, the company is poised to apply its strengths to a variety of new markets. But the company is determined to not

Exacting ISO 9001-level quality assurance makes the Dormont name synonymous with excellence.

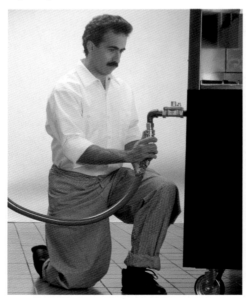

Dormont makes more stainless steel gas connectors than any other firm worldwide.

lose focus on its core business, according to President Evan Segal, whose grandfather started Dormont shortly after World War II.

In 1946, Sydney Winikoff opened a custom pipe-bending operation in Pittsburgh's Lawrenceville section. It was to be a temporary site—used only until the company could transfer its operations to the nearby suburb of Dormont, from which the company took its name. But the move never occurred, and by the early '90s, when the company relocated to its current home in Westmoreland County Industrial Park, Dormont had become the world's most widely recognized and respected name in its field.

Until the early 1970s, most commercial kitchens were built using hard metal gas pipes to connect their cooking equipment. For private homes, flexible brass hoses—used to connect furnaces, water heaters and gas dryers to stationary gas lines—were in high demand. But those

brass connectors were subject to corrosion and leaks. So Dormont stopped carrying the product line. In 1971, Chairman Jerry Segal introduced the world's first flexible, stainless steel gas connectors. Today, Dormont makes more stainless steel gas connectors than any other firm worldwide.

Demanding ISO 9001-level quality assurance and reinvestment in every aspect of the business have made Dormont synonymous with the products it makes. In the food service industry, where kitchen architects routinely specify movable cooking appliances, Dormont's flexible quick-disconnect gas hoses have now become standard.

Dormont is the exclusive supplier of gas connectors to most of America's major restaurant chains. Whenever a chain opens a new restaurant overseas, Dormont connectors almost always travel with it. The company's products reach its customers through a sophisticated distribution system including equipment and appliance manufacturers and dealers, plumbing and HVAC supply wholesalers, appliance stores, and gas utilities.

But it is the human side of Dormont's business that Jerry and Evan Segal take greatest pride in. The company maintains a full- time corporate trainer on staff. Every employee receives at least 25 hours of training a year. "We believe in continuous improvement and investing in our future. We're a company committed to its people, and that not only means our own employees, it also means our vendors and our customers," Mr. Segal said. "We're doing the things that create value for everyone." **Pa**

Westmoreland Health System and Westmoreland Regional Hospital

K eeping pace with advances in medical technology while remaining in touch with the community have been the dual challenges of Westmoreland Health System. A combination regional medical center and community health care provider, Westmoreland Health System offers leading-edge health care through its six subsidiaries while maintaining a neighborly atmosphere of caring.

The oldest and largest subsidary of the health system is Westmoreland Regional Hospital, with more than 100 years of service to Westmoreland County. "One of our greatest strengths is the high-quality, community-based health system we have developed," explained Joseph J. Peluso, president and chief executive officer, Westmoreland Health System and Westmoreland Regional Hospital. "We have expanded and added new services at the hospital and throughout the system in response to the needs of our community."

A case in point is the Heartcenter—the only comprehensive cardiac care program in Westmoreland County. Begun in 1991, the hospital opened its cardiac catheterization laboratory, with open-heart surgery following in 1992. Until that time, Westmoreland residents had to travel to Pittsburgh to receive these life-saving procedures. A Chest Pain Emergency Center and four-phase cardiac rehabilitation program are also

In addition to traditional medical and surgical care, Westmoreland opened the Heartcenter in 1991, offering comprehensive cardiac care.

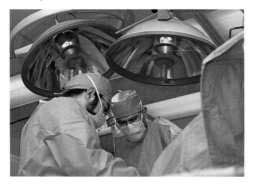

among the services forming the Heartcenter.

Another hospital service, Westmoreland for Women, provides comprehensive care for women of all ages both in and outside the hospital. For expectant mothers alone, the services range from pre-pregnancy counseling through delivery, and continuing on with infant and child care. The hospital features labor-delivery- recovery suites as well as traditional operating suites for emergencies, Cesarean section deliveries or high-risk births. The level II intensive care nursery allows ill or premature infants to receive advanced care close to home.

Cancer is a daunting and overwhelming disease. To help patients facing this challenge, Westmoreland Regional Hospital's Cancer Care Center offers specialized treatment including surgery, radiation therapy, and chemotherapy as well as access to national clinical trials and support services. Free cancer screenings are available throughout the year.

Other services include the Comprehensive Counseling Center, Sleep Disorders Center, Diabetes Treatment Center, Westmoreland Home Health Care, Westmoreland Hospice, Skilled Care Center, Barclay Rehabilitation Center, Breast Health Center, and an expanding range of geriatric services. At its core is a large inpatient unit offering traditional medical/surgical care, emergency care, and a critical care unit featuring in-house physician-specialist coverage 24 hours a day.

Maintaining the well-being of the community's healthy population is also a part of the health system mission.

Westmoreland Regional Hospital is the oldest and largest hospital in Westmoreland County.

Westmoreland Regional Hospital HEALTHPLACE, located in Westmoreland Mall, Greensburg, serves as a community health education and resource center for the community.

Other Westmoreland Health System subsidiaries are CareGivers of Southwestern Pennsylvania, a private duty registry; The SurgiCenter at Ligonier, specializing in outpatient ophthalmic procedures, laser surgery, and pain management treatments; MedCare Equipment Co., carrying medical supplies/equipment for sale or rent; Westmoreland Regional Hospital Foundation, collecting contributions to support hospital services; and Westmoreland Primary Health Center, a convenient, county-wide network of primary care physicians.

"We will strive to stay abreast of medical technology while continuing to serve our community," Mr. Peluso pledged. **Pa**

Central Westmoreland Chamber of Commerce

If the real measure of an organization's quality is its people, then the extraordinary accomplishments of the Central Westmoreland Chamber of Commerce speak well for its more than 800 members. "Our members are the driving force behind the Chamber," said Chamber president Thomas L. Sochacki, in explaining his organization's long list of achievements.

"We have high-quality individuals that provide us with a vast number of resources, skills and talents."

The Mission of the Central Westmoreland Chamber is threefold: improving the area's quality of life, strengthening its economic foundation, and serving the needs of the membership. The CWCC accomplishes the above by working hand-in-hand with the Central Westmoreland Development Corporation, with which it collaborates in expanding the area's economy. Workforce development is a particularly high priority according to Mr. Sochacki. As a member of the School-to-Work partnership, the Chamber helps to build cooperative arrangements between the business and educational communities that provides both students and teachers

New business is celebrated by the Chamber's Ambassador Committee, volunteer business leaders who roll out the red carpet for a strong economic future.

The Greensburg Train Station building, an historic landmark, is today's site of an AMTRAC Station, professional office suites, and a restaurant and micro-brewery.

with the ability to experience the working environment of today's businesses.

Not surprisingly, the leaders of the Central Westmoreland Chamber of Commerce are also the leaders in other aspects of community life. Cultivating and extending that leadership into the future is an ongoing goal of the Chamber. To help, the CWCC and the Latrobe Area Chamber of Commerce combined their individual Leadership Development Programs into a joint program called Leadership Westmoreland. Its purpose is to develop a network of community leaders capable of moving the region forward.

By exposing individuals to the know-how and experience of today's community leaders, the program not only strengthens Westmoreland County, it also builds new leadership for years to come.

The continuing growth of Central Westmoreland County's economy is another focus of the Chamber's efforts. The area's outstanding schools, safe streets, attractive communities, and excellent employment opportunities have already triggered substantial

growth. But there is always room for improvement. By making information about the area's demographics, cultural resources, historical attractions, and industrial opportunities available to interested visitors and prospective investors on demand, the Chamber bolsters healthy economic growth.

Formulating a practical vision for the area's future is another key objective. Through its wide range of programmed activities, the Chamber provides a forum where community leaders can share their ideas about the future with the Chamber's members. Short-term and long-range plans then grow from these beginnings—plans that keep the Chamber and its members focused on the future.

In the pursuit of its mission, the Chamber has also launched a web site—www.westmorelandpa.com—to showcase the area's abundant scenic, historic, cultural, and commercial resources as well as its current programs.

The Chamber initiated the creation of a Westmoreland Business Magazine called *Impact* for the Greater Greensburg Area. *Impact* contains articles addressing both Business and Community topics that are of interest to the general public and the business community.

Whether designing long-range plans and goals for the future or providing young people with an opportunity to learn about careers, the Central Westmoreland County Chamber of Commerce leverages the strengths of its large and diversified membership on behalf of all the community's residents. ▣

Westmoreland County Industrial Development Corporation

B usinesses seeking sites for expansion in Southwestern Pennsylvania want to be able to move quickly with building construction and occupancy. Delays caused by site permitting, utility extensions, and road construction can many times dissuade a company from locating at a particular site or community. No one understands this more clearly than the Westmoreland County Industrial Development Corporation, a non-profit corporation created in 1983 by the county's Board of Commissioners.

Although the WCIDC's charter covers a wide range of business development activities, its primary mission remains focused on creating ready-to-build sites in industrial parks as well as move-in-ready buildings. With properties ranging from individual leased offices for small startup firms at one extreme, to custom sites involving hundreds of acres and complex infrastructure improvements at the other, WCIDC provides sites suitable for companies of every sort and at every phase of their business life.

Since 1983, the WCIDC has opened eight industrial parks in widely separated areas of the county. Already, three of those parks are completely filled. Companies operating in these parks include firms with fewer than 10 employees as well as others with more than 400.

Westmoreland County Industrial Park III

Altogether, more than 3,700 men and women work in the WCIDC park network, and their numbers are growing rapidly.

In some cases, these industrial parks are built near the site of an established industrial organization, providing just-in-time delivery and a home for other supplier companies. The Sony Electronics operation is one such anchor. WCIDC's Technology Park, a newly-developed 112-acre property, is immediately adjacent to the Sony site. The Alcoa Research Center is another such base. WCIDC's Business and Research Park, which was built on land purchased from Alcoa in 1991, enjoys direct access to the world's largest aluminum research facility.

As the lead agency for a cluster of nonprofit organizations targeting different aspects of the county's economic development, the WCIDC works closely with other entities

including Westmoreland County's Planning Department, its Redevelopment Authority and various independent economic development agencies—entities whose missions involve specific tasks or sections of the county. The Governor's office, whose capital budgets finance many of the WCIDC's property purchases and improvements, is also a key player in the agency's development efforts.

Beyond securing land and building the infrastructure needed to make it suitable for lease or purchase, the WCIDC also carries out a series of related roles. Promoting the county to attract new businesses, collecting and distributing business information, securing cooperation among public and private sector organizations, and brokering specialized training for job-specific needs with local educational institutions are among the agency's wide-ranging responsibilities.

Today, as evidenced by the county's flourishing industrial community, the Westmoreland County Industrial Development Corporation is succeeding at all of those assignments.

Monessen Riverfront Redevelopment Park

Bibliography

Baldwin, Leland D. *Whiskey Rebels: The Story of a Frontier Uprising.* University of Pittsburgh Press, Pittsburgh, 1967.

Buck, Solon J. and Elizabeth Hawthorn. *The Planting of Civilization in Western Pennsylvania.* University of Pittsburgh Press, Pittsburgh, 1939.

Espenshade, A. Howry. *Pennsylvania Place Names.* Genealogical Publishing Co., Baltimore, 1970.

Pennsylvania Cavalcade. Compiled by the Pennsylvania Writers' Project. University of Pennsylvania Press, Philadelphia, 1942.

Swetnam, George, and Smith, Helene. *A Guidebook to Historic Western Pennsylvania.* University of Pittsburgh Press, Pittsburgh, 1976.

Wallace, Paul A.W. *Pennsylvania: Seed of a Nation.* Harper & Row, New York, 1962.

Acknowledgements

I am indebted to a number of people and organizations who gave me their time, assistance, and information and without whom this book never could have been completed.

My most grateful thanks to the people in charge of the region's economic development organizations and their staffs: Dennis H. Troy of Allegheny County and Stephen G. Leeper of the City of Pittsburgh, Richard L. Palilla of Armstrong County, James Palmer of Beaver County, Art G. Cordwell of Butler County, Michael W. Krajovic of Fayette County, Ernest Closser of Greene County, Thomas Bayuzik of Indiana County, Richard L. Ross and Therese C. McShea of Lawrence County, Malcolm Morgan of Washington County, and Larry J. Larese of Westmoreland County.

My special thanks to Roberta G. Wilson of the Pennsylvania Department of Labor and Industry for her persistent and very patient help in supplying and interpreting employment and census data, Lawrence Maloney, managing director of the Association of Iron and Steel Engineers, who provided insightful comments and suggested the focus of this book, and Carol Brown, president of the Pittsburgh Cultural Trust.

The staffs of the Greater Pittsburgh Convention and Visitors Bureau, the counties' tourism/visitors agencies and chambers of commerce all most helpfully provided volumes of historical and promotional materials. And the staffs of the Oakmont (PA) Carnegie Library and the Carnegie Library of Pittsburgh proved again and again that they are the most helpful and patient researchers and information gatherers/providers to be found anywhere.

— *Vince Gagetta*

Advertisers Index

Index